Join the Insanity

CRAZY-FUN LIFE IN THE PASTORS' WIVES CLUB

Rhonda Rhea

NEW HOPE
P U B L I S H E R S
Gospel-Centered. Missions-Driven.

BIRMINGHAM, ALABAMA

Other New Hope books
by Rhonda Rhea

How Many Lightbulbs Does It Take to Change a Person?
Bright Ideas for Delightful Transformation

Espresso Your Faith: 30 Shots of God's Word to
Keep You Focused on Christ

New Hope® Publishers
PO Box 12065
Birmingham, AL 35202-2065
NewHopeDigital.com
New Hope Publishers is a division of WMU®.

Library of Congress Product Control Number: 2013055338

Unless otherwise noted, Scripture quotations are taken from the Holman Christian Standard Bible © copyright 2000 by Holman Bible Publishers. Used by permission.

Scripture quotations marked CEV are taken from the Contemporary English Version. Copyright © 1995 American Bible Society.

Scripture quotations marked AMP are taken from the Amplified® Bible, Copyright © 1954, 1958, 1962, 1964, 1965, 1987 by The Lockman Foundation. Used by permission.

Scripture quotations marked ESV are from The Holy Bible, English Standard Version, copyright © 2001 by Crossway Bibles, a division of Good News Publishers. Used by permission. All rights reserved.

Scripture quotations marked KJV are taken from The Holy Bible, King James Version.

Scripture quotations marked *The Message* are taken from *The Message* by Eugene H. Peterson. Copyright © 1993, 1994, 1995, 1996, 2000, 2001, 2002. Used by permission of NavPress Publishing Group.

Scripture quotations marked NASB are taken from the New American Standard Bible®, Copyright © 1960, 1962, 1963, 1968, 1971, 1972, 1973, 1975, 1977, 1995 by The Lockman Foundation. Used by permission.

Scripture quotations marked NIV are taken from the HOLY BIBLE, NEW INTERNATIONAL VERSION®. NIV®. Copyright©1973, 1978, 1984 by Biblica, Inc.® Used by permission. All rights reserved.

Scripture quotations marked NLT are taken from the Holy Bible, New Living Translation, copyright © 1996. Used by permission of Tyndale House Publishers, Inc., Wheaton, Illinois. All rights reserved.

Scripture quotations marked NCV are taken from the New Century Version®. Copyright © 1987, 1988, 1991 by Word Publishing, a division of Thomas Nelson, Inc. Used by permission. All rights reserved.

Scripture quotations marked NLV are taken from the HOLY BIBLE, NEW LIFE VERSION, Copyright © 1969, 1976, 1978, 1983, 1986, Christian Literature International, P. O. Box 777, Canby OR 97013. Used by permission.

ISBN-10: 1-59669-397-5
ISBN-13: 978-1-59669-397-5

N144106• 0214 • 3M1

Cover designer: Michel Le
Interior designer: Glynese Northam

Dedication

TO OLIVIA CHRISTY, SOON-TO-BE OLIVIA Rhea. Thank you for sharing your heart—even all the uncertainties connected to entering life as a pastor's wife. And thanks for having your heart set on entering anyway. You beautifully remind me why I wrote this book. It's my delight, my blessing, to watch you become the p-dub of my son.

Contents

Acknowledgments

AS EVER AND ALWAYS, HUGE thanks, hugs, and kisses to my hubby and hero, the man who made me a p-dub all those years ago and who makes my world spin in a joyously positive direction still today, Richie Rhea. Most amazing pastor—most amazing man—I've ever known. I don't know how I would make it without your love, encouragement, and support.

Thank-yous to the rest of my extremely cool fam: Andy Rhea; Jordan Rhea; Kaley Rhea; Allie Rhea McMullin and her sweet hubby, Derek McMullin. Also to Daniel Rhea, a special and energetic thanks for the highly caffeinated book fuel in the form of coffee shop gift cards—and by energetic, I mean something close to palpitations.

Sincere thanks to Amber Lynn Guerrero for photography and marketing helps and to Jerry and Kathy Tharp for creative consultations. Who doesn't love crazy, late-night brainstorming?

Deepest appreciation to Christian Television Network's KNLJ in Jefferson City, Missouri, and especially to general manager Vickie Davenport for partnering in ministry in all kinds of imaginative and fun directions—and especially for partnering in such a sweet, Jesus-filled friendship. Love and hugs!

Special tech-shaped thank-yous to Chris Gardner, Jacob Easterday, Allie Rhea McMullin, Jordan Rhea, and Andy Rhea for the oh-so-helpful work/counsel/support. And more big thanks to Ken Klassy, whose techy contributions are always invaluable and whose web help keeps us up and running.

Hugs and heartfelt gratitude to publisher Andrea Mullins and to Joyce Dinkins, Maegan Roper, Bruce Watford, Tina

Atchenson, Glynese Northam, Melissa Hall, and all the talented and amazing, missions-minded folks at New Hope Publishers. What a team! I'm extraordinarily blessed to partner with you all in ministry.

I'm so thankful for my favorite agent of all time, Pamela Harty, who shares my heart for ministry. I'm also thankful for the helpful people at The Knight Agency who help make it possible for me to do what I love to do.

Many thanks once again to Josh Uecker at New Life 91.9 in Charlotte, North Carolina (newlife919.com), for the continued on-air insanity, and for giving so much material—a sort of test run.

Additional thank-yous to my good friends and fellow laborers at *The Pathway,* the Missouri Baptist Convention's official news journal (mbcpathway.com); *The St. Louis Metro-Voice* (metrovoice.net); *The Christian Pulse* (thechristianpulse .com); *Living Light News* in Edmonton, Alberta, Canada (livinglightnews.org); *Gospel Roads* magazine (gospelroads .com); *SBC LIFE* magazine (sbclife.org); and *HomeLife* maga-zine (lifeway.com/homelife). Thank you for giving me column space for all kinds of nonsense—and for kindly supporting me in resharing some of that nonsense in this book.

Nods of special thanks to AWSA, the Advanced Writers and Speakers Association, my heart-sisters who share support, knowledge, godly insights, and powerful prayers.

And more head-bobs of thanks to my church family at Troy First Baptist Church for consistent prayers and encouragement.

My amazing prayer team—wonderful warrior women! My sincere gratitude to you all for keeping this project bathed in prayer: Janet Bridgeforth, Tina Byus, Diane Campbell, Mary Clark, Theresa Easterday, Chris Hendrickson, Melinda Massey, and Peanuts Rudolph. I so cherish these women.

And much gratitude to the charter members of the P-Dub Club, whose contributions—written and filmed—have added such power, practicality, and pizzazz to this book: Betsy Bartig, Robin Bryce, Diane Campbell, Bobbye Cutshall, Joyce Dinkins, Sandee Hedger, Jamie Hitt, Sharon Hoffman, Cynthia Hopkins, Nicole Hufty, Kelly Lightfoot, Deb Mashburn, Robin McCall, Janet McGlaughlin, Lori Moody, Paula Mowery, Mary Englund Murphy, Diane Nix, Katie Orr, Deanna Self, Stephanie Shott, Kathy Tharp, Charlyn Thomasson, Teri Lynne Underwood, and Dawn Wilson. Love my p-dub buds!

My deepest gratitude is ever reserved to the One who saved me by His amazing grace, then saw fit to send me on this marvelous, miraculous, and often manic p-dub adventure. He sent me on the adventure, yes, but I am never on the adventure alone. To my Lord and Savior, Jesus Christ,

Thank You for Your constant presence all along the way, for Your grace, Your mercy, Your empowering, and Your indescribable love.

CHAPTER 1

An Intro: Me, My Role, and I

I'M A "P-DUB." IT'S THE slangish nickname form of PW, which is an acronym for pastor's wife. If you want in on the full etymology, I think it probably has its origins in Latin. No wait. Since I'm making this whole thing up, let's make it Hebrew—maybe Greek. It sounds more spiritual that way.

You know what's a little sad? It's sad that there are a lot of women who are automatically intimidated by me because I'm a minister's wife, which of course makes me automatically "more spiritual" than the next person, right? Oh. My. But the reason it's all so sad is that after they've spent a little time getting to know me—and it doesn't even really take all that long—they're not intimidated anymore. Not in the slightest. Sigh.

Isn't it funny, though, that the instant we join the P-Dub Club, it changes the way some people see us? Some give us credit we haven't earned. Others judge us a little more harshly than we deserve. Right now, for instance, I'm sternly judging every pastor's wife reading this who can't play the piano. Then again, I don't play the piano either. I can play "Heart and Soul," but in 30 years of ministry I can't remember even one time someone needed me to plug that into a worship service.

This is not exactly how a cool and classy p-dub would introduce a book, but while I'm confessing my own disqualifications for membership in the club, I'll go ahead and tell you that I never bring extravagantly prepared dishes to the potluck dinners. Seriously, I don't even know what a *pressure cooker* is. Some churches call them pot "bless" dinners. But if I brought a homemade dish, I'll tell you right now, it would no longer be a blessing—or even luck (if I believed in luck). So I've learned over the years that, hey, somebody needs to bring the Oreos. The kids all love me. Plus, most of the time I bring a few bags of potato chips or some other "vegetable" like that to round it out.

People often comment, "You're not like any other pastor's wife I've ever met," as they peer at me through just one eye. I never know whether I should thank them or apologize.

I'm excited about this book because in here—in the P-Dub Club—we get to relax. We get to encourage each other, laugh together, and commiserate a little. We also get to inspire each other to listen to *all* the counsel in God's Word, *some* of the counsel we hear from others (sloughing off the rest), and simply follow hard after God.

THE PERFECT P-DUB

It's always good to remember that we are who we are because of Jesus. The perfect pastor's wife? I'm sure I don't need to tell you that I'm not her. But I've never really met her either. Some have come annoyingly close (that's a joke—mostly). The good news is that I don't have to be her. You don't either. Our identity as pastor's or minister's wife is an honor we can wear, and sometimes it's a burden we bear. But who you are is never the "who" of what makes you "you." If our identity is entirely wrapped up in who we are as a minister's wife, we'll almost always find ourselves coming down heavily on the side of pride, puffed up with a skewed view of our spirituality. Or we'll come down heavily on the self-deprecating, inadequate side, knowing we'll never be all that we need to be and never feeling up to the task.

When we get to heaven, I don't think our name tags will say *Pastor's Wife* on them anywhere. I think the name tag will likely just read *His*.

Knowing *pastor's wife* will not be a label we bear for all eternity eases the pressure to be someone we're not. It balances us out when we're a little too full of ourselves. It helps the bumps in the road make a little more sense and the challenges more worth it. It eases guilt in our failures and helps us understand and more completely celebrate the victories.

It's also good to remember that the Father doesn't lump us all into one big p-dub tub. By His creative plan, we're all so incredibly unique. As different as I am from the typical pastor's wife, He's not only OK with it, He planned it. And God doesn't judge me by the successful counseling I've done—or the unsuccessful counseling. He doesn't judge me by the covered dish I bring—or don't bring. He doesn't judge me by how many committees I've chaired or whether or not I'm directing Vacation Bible School this year. He doesn't judge me by how many people I've disappointed or how many times I haven't measured up to the church's p-dub ideal. He doesn't even judge me by whether or not I can play the piano. I believe it's with great love that He looks at me and says, "You're not like any other pastor's wife I've ever made."

NOT JUST SURVIVING — THRIVING!

My desire is to grow in my role as a p-dub. We don't have to merely endure life as a minister's wife. It's not just about surviving. We can thrive! What an honor that the Lord has chosen this role for us! I want to grow in all my other roles as well. I want to continually improve in how I love my husband and my children, my church, and my neighbors. Most of all, I want to grow in how, through it all, I love my Lord.

That will be our target as we have a little fellowship through this p-dub's book. No clubbing you over the head with guilt—you can find plenty of that in other places. This is not that kind of "club." We'll have some chuckles together, and we'll look to the Word of God for what we truly need to know to grow into all we want to be.

If you would like to make *Join the Insanity* part of your devotional time, there will be some postscripts at the end of each chapter in the form of Passages to Plug In, Ponderings to Pose, and Petitions to Pray. And just so you know, we're all on this journey together. So thanks for coming along.

While I will no doubt continue to find new ways to disqualify myself from the club, I will also continue to bask in His unlimited grace and His extravagant mercy. And I'll just decide to appreciate the fact that at least I don't intimidate any of you.

P-DUB TO P-DUB

Let's face it, ministry wives don't have all that many opportunities to get together. But isn't it therapeutic when we do connect? I could have written a group study for this book, but I know all you p-dubs are busy up to your eyebrows in your own family, church ministries, and all the rest. Instead, I thought we could have one of those "next best thing" connections. Each chapter includes a testimony or a tidbit of wisdom from a fellow minister's wife. These are women who truly "get" your life. And for a sort of face-to-face with that fellow p-dub, you'll find a web link to an additional message from her. Some of the videos are on the topic they've addressed in the book. Others have provided an additional message they felt was precisely for you. The vid-message from this chapter? This one's just a little word from me. Thanks for "linking" arms with others in the P-Dub Club!

P-DUB PARTNER-LINK: https://www.youtube.com /watch?feature=player_embedded&v=VZtjzkuSsiI

You can find an easy link at rhondarhea.com at the P-Dub tab.

P-DUB POSTSCRIPTS

Passages to Plug In

And this I pray: that your love may abound yet more and more and extend to its fullest development in knowledge and all keen insight [that your love may display itself in greater depth of acquaintance and more comprehensive discernment], So that you may surely learn to sense what is vital, and approve and prize what is excellent and of real value [recognizing the highest and the best, and distinguishing the moral differences], and that you may be untainted and pure and unerring and blameless [so that with hearts sincere and certain and unsullied, you may approach] the day of Christ [not stumbling nor causing others to stumble]. May you abound in and be filled with the fruits of righteousness (of right standing with God and right doing) which come through Jesus Christ (the Anointed One), to the honor and praise of God [that His glory may be both manifested and recognized] (Philippians 1:9–11 AMP).

Ponderings to Pose

Kick-starting our p-dub time together, let's look a little closer at the above passage in Philippians 1 in the Amplified Bible version. What are some ways the Lord could use this passage to balance our identity between self-focused pride and ineffective insecurity?

Petitions to Pray

Paul prayed the prayer in the highlighted passage for the Philippians and essentially for us too. Let's agree with Paul and with each other in prayer, asking the Lord to do the things listed there. Here are a handful of the points to pray:

- Lord, let my love grow more and more and "display itself in greater depth." Grow me as a pastor's wife—and in every other role You've given me.
- Father, help me sense what is vital, recognize what's best, and not give place to the rest.
- I ask that You help me to stay pure, not stumbling or causing others to stumble.
- Only You can cause my life to abound with the fruits of righteousness. May I bear fruit in Your name and for Your glory.

CHAPTER 2

Swimming in the Fishbowl— Without Sleeping with the Fishes

A life scrutinized probably won't kill us. But what do we do with all those extra eyeballs?

HOW ABOUT WE ALL JUST do this thing together? Let's simultaneously go to the pantry for something to snack on. Then let's stand and stare at a box of instant potatoes for about three minutes, unable to decide what, if anything, looks good. Incidentally, last time I stared too long, even a packet of Shake 'n Bake that may have been lurking there since the 70s started to look good.

Decisions can be tough in any decade. We all make a lot of difficult choices every day. That's why I try not to judge people, for instance, according to their snack choices. Even when they don't choose chocolate (you say potato, I say Butterfinger) or honey oat bread at Subway (because honey oat is the Butterfinger of breads). Even when I don't understand their choices *at all*.

KEEPING AN EYE ON YOU

As p-dubs, however, some decisions aren't exactly ours to make. If we could decide the number of eyeballs focused on our lives, I wonder how many we would choose. Living under constant observation from, well, everyone is one of the chief complaints among ministers' wives.

It can be daunting to go about your everyday life and ministry with a seemingly ever-present audience. I don't always want everyone knowing exactly how many Butterfingers I can put away in a week—or where I got some of them. *Why, kids, what do you mean some of your Halloween candy is missing?*

But I also know that the fishbowl life holds a lot of good potential—for us as p-dubs and for our church as well. We have unique opportunities to influence people as we live out our faith in the everydayness of life. Scary? Yes. Because we can have a good influence, or we can drop the ball from our Butterfingery hands. And when we stumble, we do it publicly, in front of a potentially large group of sometimes-harsh judges.

Our audience's accountability keeps us on our toes. Those extra eyeballs can help us keep our own eyeballs fixed on the Father, depending on Him for the strength, wisdom, and discipline we need to become a good example of following Christ, holding on to His plan with everything we've got. And even when that hold feels weak, we can sometimes have more good influence by a godly response to a mess-up than we would've been able to have if we had done things right in the first place. Confessing our weaknesses and failures, humbling ourselves, asking forgiveness, righting a wrong—those lessons may not be fun for the watcher, but they can be so valuable for everyone involved.

Alternately, sometimes we crave the attention of the eyeballs, but for all the wrong reasons. Or we become paranoid, sensing the eyes watching even when they're not.

Pastornoia, maybe? Where do we find the right attitude while living in an aquarium?

THE AGE OF AQUARIUM

Paul experienced life in the fishbowl. And he used it. He said in Philippians 4:9, "What you have learned and received and heard and seen in me — practice these things, and the God of peace will be with you" (ESV). When he mentions the things that the people had "learned" from him, he gives us a clue that he had spent time teaching them — just as your hubby or you may spend time teaching others. But he also refers to the things that his people had "received" and the things they had "heard" and, yes, even the things they had "seen" in him. More than hands-on: eyeballs on! He gave them complete freedom to scrutinize his life. The Greek word for "seen" here is *horao,* and it describes something a bit more than merely looking on. It's not just glancing. It describes observing to the point of understanding what's really happening. Paul invites his people to watch him and to let what they see change them. Paul is all but shouting to these people, "Hey! Get a load of this!" He seems to view every pair of those eyes as an opportunity. This is true for us as well: every pair of watchful eyes is an opportunity to demonstrate the power of God at work in our lives.

FISHING FOR PEACE

OK, so is anyone getting hung up on the last part of that verse? Because the last thing we tend to think of when we think of the looked-upon life is peace. But this life with an audience didn't seem to upset Paul at all. I think he was so in tune with Jesus that a scrutinized life didn't frighten him. When he told them to follow his example and that if they did, the God of peace would be with them, doesn't that mean Paul was at peace too?

We find peace in the presence of the Lord as we live in the power of His Holy Spirit—with or without the audience. Then Paul reminds us where he gets his strength in a verse we breathe in and out regularly as p-dubs: "I can do all things through Him who strengthens me" (Philippians 4:13 NASB).

Naturally our different personalities come into play in all of this. Some p-dubs welcome the spotlight and cameras into their lives. Others adjust and learn to cope with it. Still others resent it—even consider it wrong for the people in their churches to intrude with their stares. Guess what? God gives strength to women with each personality and response. And every time we decide to embrace His strength for the right kind of *watchitude*, we'll find His peace too. It's amazing that as we rest in that strength, we begin to see every stare as one more chance to let someone be an eyewitness to what the Lord is doing in our lives and in our families.

It truly is our decision. We decide if we're going to resent the watching or welcome it. And we choose whether to embrace His strength and experience His peace or to miss both. So let's make our decisions wisely, sisters. Though, for the record, regarding decisions in the pantry, after you've stared for more than 20 minutes, it becomes acceptable to eat the leftover taco shells.

P-Dub to P-Dub with SANDEE HEDGER

"Let your eyes look directly ahead, And let your gaze be fixed straight in front of you. Watch the path of your feet, and all your ways will be established" (Proverbs 4:25–26 NASB). How easy it is for us to lose focus and allow our eyes to dart from one spectator to another within our church, craving approval and affirmation while missing the pure delight in pleasing our Father.

The pastor's wife fishbowl (PWF) is both painfully real and deceptively imaginary, and sometimes both within a light-speed section of time, throwing my tender heart and fragile nerves into mass chaos and a spiritual dilemma.

Like every other pastor's wife, I can share enough stories to indict quite a crowd of bad-mannered sheep spattered across our 35 years of ministry life. I was awakened to the PWF at the tender age of 23 as I faced our first pastorate's annual holiday dinner. It's the dinner that turned into the "Do you even know how to cook a turkey?" episode. Reality was that I did not know how to roast a turkey, much less four! I was a novice . . . and busted.

We served turkey soup at that dinner. I had roasted the fiber out of those birds over the course of about 12 hours (seriously). It was an embarrassing learning experience and brutal critique but surprisingly, not needless pain. I was on the fast-track sanctification plan, and my very loving Father had chosen to place me under the scrutiny of a robust woman who gloried in "speaking frankly." I was in the PWF. It was real. But it was an assignment from my perfect Father. He desperately wanted me to learn to love and serve tough people, embracing critique, and shaking off criticism.

At the same time, it was one of many imaginary crises that screamed for preeminence in my mind, and from that, too, there were lessons Father wanted me to learn. I had not ruined His plan nor forfeited my husband's calling to ministry. His plan and calling remained and, in all reality, my path was not the same as Julia Child's. Needful lessons. Painful truths. The path to freedom in service came in learning to keep my eyes focused on *His* established path for me and my gaze fixed upon His face where approval is found.

P-DUB PARTNER-LINK: http://youtu.be/2aPbrj66YlU

You can find an easy link at rhondarhea.com at the P-Dub tab.

P-DUB POSTSCRIPTS

Passages to Plug In

You are the light of the world. A city set on a hill cannot be hidden. Nor do people light a lamp and put it under a basket, but on a stand, and it gives light to all in the house. In the same way, let your light shine before others, so that they may see your good works and give glory to your Father who is in heaven (Matthew 5:14–16 ESV).

Ponderings to Pose

"Shake 'n Bake?" That's one thing. But Sandee Hedger encourages us to "embrace and shake." What might the Lord be leading you to embrace? What could He be encouraging you to shake off? Look again at the Proverbs 4:25–26 passage Sandee shared. It's all too easy to focus on where the eyes of others are looking and forget where our own eyes should be, isn't it? According to this passage, what's in store for the ones who keep looking in the right direction?

Petitions to Pray

Let's pray the Matthew 5:14–16 "Passages to Plug In" passage above in the most personal way:

• Father, thank You for making me a light in this world.

- Give me the courage to shine it, not hide it. May You shine light on others through all that You're doing in my life.
- Lord, let Your light shine so brightly in me that others will see Your good works and give You glory.

CHAPTER 3

Positively Positive

Taking on the mind-battle to get rid of negative thinking and focus on the positives.

GLASS-HALF-FULL PERSON? Glass-half-empty person? Hm. I consider myself a pretty positive chick. Yet I tend to be more of a dribble-whatever's-in-the-glass-down-my-shirt person. It's always best if I try to coordinate whatever I'm wearing with the meal of the moment. That's one big reason that I so want a chocolate suit.

My husband? We should always buy him shirts made of ink. Spots under the pocket wouldn't be spots. They would just be, well, more shirt. They say that the clothes make the man. If that's true, Richie's clothes make him Ink Man. Yet you should know (and I'm not saying this with even a hint of sarcasm), "Ink Man" will always be my hero. He has a special "spot" in my heart.

When it comes to focusing on the positives instead of the negatives, some days in ministry are tougher than others. The nature of ministry and people who tend to drain you dry makes it so. And the negatives can be so much easier to see. I think a huge reason is because our enemy is not stupid.

He knows if he can lure you into fixating on the negatives, your spiritual life can become something close to barren. He can use aggravations from immature people, busyness, and all kinds of distractions and extreme weariness to cause everything negative to seem loud and all-consuming, while all the blessings of life seem to speak hardly above a whisper.

As wives of ministers, let's face it, because of the more public nature of how we walk out our lives with God, we're targeted. If we fall, there's greater potential for taking others with us. And once Satan gets our focus on everything negative about the church, our love for God's people and our willingness to serve them selflessly starts to fade. We're not filling anyone's glass with anything!

This is a spiritual battle, my friends. And it's a battle with your fruitfulness at stake.

In a spiritual battle, I choose to team up with those who are well-armed. The villains waging war against us in this life are heavier on the evil than any you'll find in your average superhero movie. I know you've read the words of Paul in Ephesians 6:11–12 where he tells us,

> *Put on the whole armor of God, that you may be able to stand against the schemes of the devil. For we do not wrestle against flesh and blood, but against the rulers, against the authorities, against the cosmic powers over this present darkness, against the spiritual forces of evil in the heavenly places* (ESV).

THE ARMOR MAKES THE P-DUB

Every time we try to suck it up and overcome those loud negatives in our own strength, we end up dribbling defeat down the front of our shirts. "Cosmic powers over this present darkness"? Nothing in the comics compares. Then again, nothing—imaginary or real—compares with the strength we find in the armor of God. We're able to stand against evil as we put on that armor. If Iron Man alter ego Tony Stark came strutting up to some giant supervillain without his powered suit of armor, not only would he look ridiculous but he would also be toast. I can just imagine him trying to shoot power beams out of his bare hands. Nothing. Or maybe jumping up to fly off and going nowhere. As a superhero, Tony is nakedly nothing without the suit. He's defenseless. It would be the ultimate foolishness for him to even think of going into a battle with an evil nemesis without his armor.

We are spiritually armed and battle-ready when we take off anything fleshly—all traces of self-sufficiency and those prideful thoughts that seek to deceive us into thinking we have any kind of power of our own we can carry into the fray. Ephesians 6:10 is a passage that makes it clear where our battle-readiness should come from: "Finally, be strong in the Lord and in the strength of his might" (ESV). His strength. His might. Because it's His battle. And the next verse tells us we should "put on the whole armor of God." Not of self. Not of man. Not of some kind of "positive thinking" program. Not of any of our own ideas of how superhero strength should operate. His armor.

No power on this planet or any other can prevail against us when we're armored up. No negative can outshine His positive. His truth enables us, His righteousness empowers us, His gospel of peace emboldens us, and the faith He gives us fortifies us. No need for any glass-half-full kind of thinking here. Battles fought in His strength? We can't lose. Whether it's the battle to fight negativity or the other spiritual battles we're called to fight, I'm happy to tell you in the most positive way that we're "well-suited" for each and every one.

P-Dub to P-Dub with SHARON HOFFMAN

Not too many years ago, I became so caught up in mothering teens; work responsibilities; perpetual activity at church, school, and home that I lost all joy. I am embarrassed to admit my extreme ingratitude and negativity—especially when I owe Christ such a debt for all He's done for me. I was exhausted.

"Babe, you're not very fun anymore," my husband, Rob, said gently one evening.

His words stung. I felt defensive and angry. I truly wanted my husband, of all people, to understand. His comment did, however, prove to be a turning point toward improved understanding of the negativity filling my heart and mind.

Admittedly, I needed to learn some time-management skills to address the cause of some of my stress. I spoke honestly to God about my being grumpy and negative most of the time. I began to intentionally acknowledge to myself that I didn't need to try to meet up to every church member's expectations. Resentment had filled my soul as I'd let the people-pleasing trap suck all my joy in serving.

Naked honesty with myself was a huge first step. Absolutely refusing to let negative thinking destroy me, I began replacing my sour spirit by memorizing hopeful verses in Scripture. I copied encouraging verses on 3-by-5 cards—I still do, to this day. Throughout the day I take every chance to review my cards for the day. Before long, I've hidden them in my heart.

Something else that makes a huge difference is listing five things for which I'm thankful each day. Praising and thanking God for His protection, provision, a flower, an opportunity to cheer a friend, a chai tea—all through the day I'm making my list mentally. Then at night I write my gratefulness list down.

What a jump start to joy these two practices have been in my life. They can stop your stinkin' thinkin' too!

Oh, and my Rob, as recently as last week told me, "There's no one in the world who I have more fun with than *you*!" You know I smiled from ear to ear.

P-DUB PARTNER-LINK: http://www.youtube.com/watch?v=-t3N-PDS1TU

You can find a quick link at rhondarhea.com at the P-Dub tab.

P-DUB POSTSCRIPTS

Passages to Plug In

Rejoice in the Lord always; again I will say, rejoice. Let your reasonableness be known to everyone. The Lord is at hand; do not be anxious about anything, but in everything by prayer and supplication with thanksgiving let your requests be made known to God. And the peace of God, which surpasses all understanding, will guard your hearts and your minds in Christ Jesus. Finally, brothers, whatever is true, whatever is honorable, whatever is just, whatever is pure, whatever is lovely, whatever is commendable, if there is any excellence, if there is anything worthy of praise, think about these things (Philippians 4:4–8 ESV).

Ponderings to Pose

Let's take Sharon Hoffman's testimony as a challenge. What passages might the Lord use in your life to help you focus on the positives in the power of Christ? Would you be willing to write them on 3-by-5 cards and ponder them all week long, Sharon-style? Take an inventory of the positives in your life and list at least five. Let those become more thanks-fuel and a jump start for positive joy.

Petitions to Pray

We're instructed in the "armor" passage to "Pray at all times in the Spirit" (Ephesians 6:18). Pray through each piece of the armor in Ephesians 6:14–18, asking the Lord to use each one in your life to keep you from falling into the negative schemes of the devil. These are prayers that are positively powerful!

CHAPTER 4

When There's a P-Dub Rub

Encouragement in dealing with those friction-heavy folks who seem consistently to rub us the wrong way.

WHENEVER SOMEONE IS WORKING REALLY hard to make a solid argument on an issue they're passionate about, it's easy to get frustrated. When I'm in a heated discussion, I try to avoid turning the argument around with "I'm rubber and you're glue." I know that strategy does nothing for a person's believability. But I admit it. There are people in life and ministry who just seem to know exactly what to say to bug me to the core. My response? I might opt for "takes one to know one" except that I would be insulting myself at the same time—and that seems counterproductive.

BOUNCING BLESSINGS

Using words to wound is always counterproductive. I wish I could say I've never done it. But it doesn't take long to figure out that words don't really bounce either. They can wound. And when we're bent on wounding, we miss a big opportunity to grow in character and wisdom. Proverbs 18:2

says, "A fool does not delight in understanding, but only wants to show off his opinions." Trading wisdom just to show off? Bad trade. Even if I have a superbly spiritual-sounding comeback I could show off.

Not only do we miss the opportunity for growing in understanding when we get cranky with those who aggravate us, but we also miss the blessing of being a blessing. Every time you use your words to bless someone else, they become a rubber blessing of grace that bounces right back around to stick to you.

We don't often think of Ephesians 4:29 as a passage for ministers' wives since we're already the "extraspiritual ones." But our extraspiritualness doesn't always make it all the way from our hearts to our brains—and then back to our tongues. "Let no corrupting talk come out of your mouths, but only such as is good for building up, as fits the occasion, that it may give grace to those who hear." The word *corrupting* is from a Greek word that was originally used for rotten, putrefied food. In other words, corrupt as the bag of spinach I found in my college daughter's fridge. I'm still recovering. We were digging around for salad fixings and our conversation went something like this:

ME: "Kaley, your spinach has brown juice sloshing around in the bottom of the bag."
KALEY: "Yeah, don't eat that. Also, don't eat that bacon."
ME: "No prob. I never eat bacon that . . . blue."

The smell made my eyes water a little. Major reekage. Do I even need to say that I wasn't the least bit tempted to put any of that in my mouth? How awful is it that I pay more attention to salad or anything else that goes into my mouth than I do to the words I let come out of it?

SAYS WHO?

We're told in that Ephesians passage (4:29) that we're to choose a word that "fits the occasion"—words that are just right. That brings us back to the blessing of blessing. Paul doesn't only tell us to stay away from the words that reek, but he gives us specific instructions for how our words should smell instead. When people get a whiff of my words, they should be taking in the sweet scent of grace.

It's not about what "says you." It's not about "what says me" either. It all comes back around to "says Him." Jesus Himself said, "For the mouth speaks from the overflow of the heart" (Matthew 12:34). I don't want to overflow liquefied spinach or bacon that may or may not have blinked. I want to allow Jesus so to fill my heart that my heart overflows grace words to all around.

I'll just tell you, there are days I settle for simply not verbally responding with ugly words when someone rubs me the wrong way. Maybe a lot of days. My most joy-filled days, however, are the ones where I get my brain and my heart in on the choice not to respond.

I do that when I ask the Lord to help me see people who rub me the wrong way exactly the way He sees them. It happens as I ask Him to give me a deep love for those He loves and ask Him then to love them through me—to fill every place in my heart where I'm powerless to love with His love-power. Not because these people are worthy of love, but because my Lord is more than worthy of my obedience. Loving them out of love for Him.

CHOSEN FOR THE HIGH ROAD

*God loves you and has chosen you as his own spe-
cial people. So be gentle, kind, humble, meek, and
patient. Put up with each other, and forgive anyone
who does you wrong, just as Christ has forgiven
you. Love is more important than anything else. It
is what ties everything completely together. Each one
of you is part of the body of Christ, and you were
chosen to live together in peace. So let the peace that
comes from Christ control your thoughts* (Colossians
3:12–15 CEV).

It's only by His grace that we're able to take the high road
and rise above an irritation. He calls me to love and forgive
even those who are the most annoying. And do I even have
to add that sometimes the one doing the most annoying is
me? Takes one to know one? I know that's right.

P-Dub to P-Dub with *CHARLYN THOMASSON*
In the earliest years of ministry, when it came to people who
rubbed me the wrong way, my heart and mind were on the
defense. I had what I thought were great words of wisdom at
the ready, though when I shared them, I usually felt worse.
My second line of defense was avoidance. I would actually
walk through a different entrance on Sunday mornings to
escape certain people. I was even known to quietly slip out
of meetings. I was the queen of avoidance. I know, I know
—doesn't sound very spiritual.

Focusing on what Scripture has to say about expressing
God's love to others has been changing my view of those
"rubs." Daily appointments alone with God and extended

Sabbaths have fed my heart and mind so that God's wisdom guides me in the difficulties of ministry. I'm also working to cultivate deep and close friendships with women outside my church. We hold one another accountable and sincerely pray for each other. We are completely open, honest, and vulnerable. I also have fun with these friends. Friends feed fun and fade friction!

My heart goes out to pastors' wives in the friction-heavy spots who feel hurt and frustrated. I know what that's like. I know very well the conflict of negative thoughts versus a desire to love like Jesus. I am learning more and more to view those times when people rub me the wrong way as opportunities to grow, learn, and change. A "rub" is a chance for me to understand God's unconditional love at a deeper level. Friction forces us to walk in confidence with God. During tough times God often reveals how He desires to use us uniquely to minister to others. He diminishes the inner conflict and develops the unfading beauty of a gentle and quiet spirit, which is of great worth to him (1 Peter 3:4). Only God can turn a RUB into a way to Reflect Unfading Beauty.

P-DUB PARTNER-LINK: http://youtu.be/26nzQLgFOpo

You can find an easy link at rhondarhea.com at the P-Dub tab.

P-DUB POSTSCRIPTS

Passages to Plug In

Live in harmony with one another. Do not be haughty, but associate with the lowly. Never be wise in your own sight. Repay no one evil for evil, but give thought to do what is honorable in the sight of all. If

possible, so far as it depends on you, live peaceably
with all (Romans 12:16–18 ESV).

Ponderings to Pose

Could Charlyn Thomasson's four-part process for dealing
with difficult people work for you? Can you find Scriptures
that support each of her steps?

- Focusing on what God's Word says about showing His
  love to others
- Spending extended time alone with Him
- Cultivating honest friendships/accountability partners
- Seeing every "rub" as an opportunity to grow

Petitions to Pray

Anytime there's a bit of a rub, let's be ready to pray through
these prayer points:

- Lord, take my words.
- Take my thoughts.
- Bring my words and my thoughts under Your control and
  filter them through Your love.
- Help me to remember that even that person who annoys
  me most is one You created and one You dearly love. Love
  them through me, for Your glory.

CHAPTER 5

Wounded Warrior

Annoyances are one thing. But what do we do when we're truly wounded? Embracing forgiveness, finding comfort, moving beyond the hurt.

I DON'T KNOW WHY WE'RE always making things a lot more complicated than we need to, but repairs shouldn't be rocket science. Unless you're a scientist repairing rockets. But everything else is a lot simpler than we tend to make it. According to my grandfather, if it's mechanical, you fix it with duct tape or WD-40. In extreme cases, both. According to my grandmother, if it's living, sometimes you fix it with Vicks VapoRub. Sometimes Campho-Phenique. In extreme cases, both. According to me, everything that doesn't require rocket science can most likely be fixed with chocolate. Also, for all the categories and for every fix-it need, you should always try the chocolate first.

I could be wrong, but it seems to me most civil upheaval happens in the countries with the least amount of chocolate. I think I could demonstrate my reasoning with a pie chart.

Of course, mine would be a chocolate pie chart. But that's OK because then I could make my point slice by slice.

Ah, there's the fix—the sweet life. This discovery could help protect the civility of our culture one whipped cream-covered bite at a time.

THE SWEET LIFE?

A wounded heart, though, requires an entirely different fix. Duct tape won't touch it. Vicks can't VapoRub it away. There's no physical thing on this planet that can mend a broken heart. I've heard so many ministry wives testify through tears that the biggest surprise of life in the ministry has been how very "unsweet" Christians can be. Many thought that loving these people would be easy as pie, so to speak. I'm not talking about the annoyances we're called to rise above. I'm talking about the cruel attacks that wound us to our very core.

WHAT DO WE DO WITH OVERWHELMING PAIN?

If you're experiencing that kind of pain right now, let me first say I'm so sorry you're in the midst of such heartache. I know that feeling. And I'll tell you plainly, I hate it.

And now, could I tell you something that might be a little difficult to hear? It's this: We are called to a different standard when it comes to dealing with hurtful people. Not because we're pastor's wives—though I do think we have a calling to a high standard as p-dubs—but simply because the Father has made it clear how His children are to respond. We're to answer with forgiveness. And we're even called to respond a step or two beyond merely forgiving. Paul instructs in Romans 12,

> *Bless those who persecute you; bless and do not curse*
> *them. . . . Repay no one evil for evil, but give thought*
> *to do what is honorable in the sight of all. If possible,*
> *so far as it depends on you, live peaceably with all.*
> *Beloved, never avenge yourselves, but leave it to the*
> *wrath of God, for it is written, "Vengeance is mine,*
> *I will repay, says the Lord." To the contrary, "if your*
> *enemy is hungry, feed him; if he is thirsty, give him*
> *something to drink; for by so doing you will heap burn-*
> *ing coals on his head." Do not be overcome by evil, but*
> *overcome evil with good* (vv. 14, 17–21 ESV).

Blessing instead of cursing—when, let's face it, the person really deserves a cursing. Blessing is not the easy way. We'd rather get even. That person hurt you? Hurt him back! But we're not called to the easy way. We're called to forgive. And then—are you ready for this?—to go beyond even that, and to bless. To show love. To a person's ugliness, or downright evil, with good.

BUT I DON'T WANNA

I admit it. In my flesh, that's the last thing I want. When someone's been a jerk, he doesn't deserve a blessing. There's no way I can show goodness and kindness and love on my own. It takes a power so very beyond me.

It's a miraculously beautiful thing when the Lord calls us to do something we can't do, and then He does it for us and through us, isn't it? I've experienced it. I've seen it in others. I can tell you, He is faithful. If you will trust Him, He will give you the ability, the strength, to love in every way you can't.

Then Christ will make his home in your hearts as you trust in him. Your roots will grow down into God's love and keep you strong. . . . May you experience the love of Christ, though it is too great to understand fully. Then you will be made complete with all the fullness of life and power that comes from God (Ephesians 3:17, 19 NLT).

THE PAIN-FIX

So what about the pain? What happens to it? It's true, no physical thing on this planet can mend a broken heart. But ultimately Jesus has exactly the fix we need to make every hurting place bearable. Deep down in our souls, we know that's true. Sometimes we have to let our souls remind our hurting hearts. We need to just sit still for a minute, even in the pain, and just know it.

This doesn't mean the pain will automatically disappear. One thing I remember clearly about Campho-Phenique. When my grandma put it on a skinned knee, it stung. There still may be that same kind of lingering sting. But we can have the victory if we embrace forgiveness and refuse to give in to bitterness.

You've probably counseled dozens of women who have let bitterness poison their lives. We can't think for a second that the same thing can't happen to us. Bitterness darkens our heart and kills our usefulness—sometimes even our husbands' effectiveness in ministry. The poison can seep its way into our home all the way into our relationships with our children. We simply can't let that dark poison have even the smallest place in our lives.

FINDING COMFORT, MOVING ON

We also can't forget for a second that Jesus understands being wounded. He understands being punished for something He didn't do. He understands betrayal—with a Judas kiss, no less. There's great comfort in resting in the Savior who understands, and there's great comfort in allowing His immense love to ease every sting.

In the end, the Lord God will right every wrong, whether we get to see it or not. May I encourage you not to focus so much on defending yourself or proving you're right, but rather on showing off how great our God is? When we're attacked, we have a reflexive desire to counterattack. We come up with excellent arguments, making speeches—in real life and some-times in our minds—to prove ourselves just.

When our minds are full of those arguments, we can't move on. Sometimes convincing people we're right is not the important issue. What's important is allowing Him to be what we need, to love and forgive and bless someone who is undeserving. It's not as vital to prove we're right as it is to make sure we're right before our Lord. Are we loving Him? Are we allowing Him to love others through us? When all is said and done, that's what will count.

There's such delight in trusting Him, relishing His comfort and moving on in obedience. It's how to make it victoriously through your season of pain. Sting or no sting, whipped cream or no whipped cream, this is where we'll find the sweet life.

P-Dub to P-Dub with KELLY LIGHTFOOT

I would love to tell you a juicy story full of devastation, darkness, and . . . well, a near excommunication. And this true story would play out just like one of those spy movies where it seems all the good guys turn out to be bad guys, and that spy guy is left trying to get out alive, though he can no longer trust anyone. But what I really want to share is the ending—that's the best part. That's when the strong arm of our loving Father reached into my life and held tightly to me despite the constant confusion and overwhelming disorientation of that long season. Lyrics from my favorite song describe this truth so well:

> From life's first cry to final breath,
> Jesus commands my destiny.
> No pow'r of hell, no scheme of man,
> Can ever pluck me from His hand.

One night, when the unexpected and hopeless season of life finally climaxed into glorious daylight, I realized that when I can make sense of nothing, when loneliness presses in, and when I am helpless to mend shattered relationships, I am still His daughter. My salvation has already been purchased. I am sealed by his blood. I am still His daughter, and He loves me unconditionally.

P-DUB PARTNER-LINK: http://www.youtube.com/watch?v=_bvBfnpjafU
    You can find an easy link at rhondarhea.com at the P-Dub tab.

P-DUB POSTSCRIPTS

Passages to Plug In

Do not grieve the Holy Spirit of God, by whom you were sealed for the day of redemption. Let all bitterness and wrath and anger and clamor and slander be put away from you, along with all malice. Be kind to one another, tender-hearted, forgiving each other, just as God in Christ also has forgiven you (Ephesians 4:30–32 NASB).

Ponderings to Pose

Kelly Lightfoot understands hurt and betrayal. Her comfort came as she dwelt on the fact that she was still safely tucked into the Lord's hand and that no one could pluck her out. She knew beyond a doubt that she could rest in knowing that, no matter what, she is His treasured daughter. Psalm 4:3 (NLT) says, "You can be sure of this: The Lord set apart the godly for himself. The Lord will answer when I call to him." We can be "sure." No doubt. When His child calls, the Father hears. And He responds. And even when His response is nothing like what we have in mind, we can trust Him. His answer is big. It's eternal. It takes into account eternity past and eternity future, without forgetting the right now. Trust His perfect will. And trust Him to hold you up when it's not what you had in mind. Rest in the sure knowledge that you are special to Him. Just as He has set you apart, He will hold you together.

Petitions to Pray

In the verses from Ephesians in the Passages to Plug In, it's clear that bitterness grieves the Spirit of God. And it can escalate into slander and all kinds of violence if it's not mastered. Ask the Lord right now to take away any bitterness and give you what you need to forgive and love instead. You may have to pray the prayer again before the day is over. And maybe again in the morning. That's OK. Pray it every time you sense the bitterness sneaking back in. Then watch as the Lord gives you the ability even to pray that your offender will be blessed. His love is that miraculous!

CHAPTER 6

Fixing a P-Dub Flub

An epic fail. We've all had one. Failures and shortcomings that actually bless others? Totally possible. There is mercy. And there is victory.

I'M SO GLAD I NEVER make stupid mistakes. I'm a pastor's wife, you know. We're not allowed to be stupid.

Wow. You should be really proud of me. I typed all that with a straight face. I'm laughing uproariously at myself now though. While I'm laughing, maybe this would be a good spot to tell you the "What Do I Do with Myself Now That I'm Perfect?" chapter comes later. Later . . . as in the next life.

The truth is, I have so many fluff-brained moments in everyday life and ministry it's not even funny. Wait, it usually *is* funny. And I guess that's probably how I became a humor writer. So there is that.

NOW WHERE DID I LEAVE THAT BRAIN?

I had another one of those fluffy-headed days recently. I'm pretty sure I set my brain on top of my car and then drove off with it still up there. Come to think of it, I wonder how many things I've left on top of the car over the years. I lose more coffee that way! I call it "road-spill." I'm thinking of putting a cupholder up there. Problem solved.

And coffee isn't the only thing flying off car roofs—so many cell phones, dying so young. My husband gave his the double whammy. He didn't even need the car roof. He put his phone in his gym bag, then forgot and left the bag *behind* his car. In case you've ever wondered, your phone can sometimes survive you backing over it with your car. But don't expect it to keep kickin' if, after you take it out of the bag, you accidentally drop it into your cup of coffee. That was a bad phone day *and* a bad coffee day. A bad car day, really.

AND WHERE DID I LEAVE THAT CART?

I would tease Richie about this incident, except that just a few weeks ago I had a bad *cart* day. I was pushing around a cart-full of groceries at the store and ran into a couple from church. The husband looked down at the gargantuan hunk of chocolate in my cart with a raised eyebrow and said, "Is that Richie's?" I said, in a voice that thoroughly betrayed my own surprise, "No. But it's not mine either!" When I looked over the rest of the contents of my cart, I realized none of that stuff was mine. Including the purse sitting in the cart seat. Lordy, mercy. I had accidentally rolled off with somebody else's cart!

By the time I made it back to where I thought I probably made the accidental switch, the lady whose cart I had "stolen" already had the manager waiting for me.

O Lord. Please don't let them use the cuffs.

Every potential headline that I imagined in that split second had the words *pastor's wife* in it. Which didn't fit well with the *larceny* I imagined along with it. Or *penitentiary*.

I groveled apologetically while she checked to make sure I hadn't pilfered any of her credit cards. So embarrassing. I tried to make a few jokes—told her I left my purse there as collateral, even—but she never cracked a smile. At least she didn't send me to jail. Although even though it's been several weeks, I'll still be extra nervous if I see a law enforcement officer on my front porch. It's troubling that if they accuse me of making off with the lady's purse, it'll be an accusation I can't even deny.

One thing I'm never accused of: being the perfect pastor's wife.

TAKING A DIFFERENT KIND OF SPILL

It must be killer pressure to try to keep up a fake face of perfection. If you're trying it, let me set you free with a couple of truthful tidbits: (1) You're not perfect; you're going to make mistakes. (2) That's OK because, in reality, you don't have to be perfect.

As a matter of fact, sometimes people are actually relieved to find out their minister's wife is human. Granted, some of us are a bit more "human" than others. But I can honestly tell you that at every point I've confessed my extreme humanness, my weaknesses and failures—almost without exception—I've been shown grace. I know that doesn't always happen, but I think God honors our openness and honesty either way.

In those times when others don't show grace, God still does. "But he gives more grace. Therefore it says, 'God opposes the proud, but gives grace to the humble' . . . Humble yourselves before the Lord, and he will exalt you" (James 4:6, 10 ESV).

While He opposes the proud, God has grace ready for the humble. I think a lot of people tend to do the same. When someone humbly admits a fail, most Christians respond with a heart to comfort and restore. They don't usually feel the need to further humiliate you when you're already groveling. But the person who refuses to admit a wrong? There's often a feeling—even though it's not the best response—that there's a need to convince you of your failure until you *are* humble. If we humble ourselves, then maybe someone else won't feel so strongly that they need to do it for us.

THERE'S A FAIL, AND THEN THERE'S A MORE EPIC FAIL

Incidentally, it's one thing when our brains are giving us the silent treatment and there's a faux pas or some kind of accidental blunder. And we still have to deal with those situations with grace—and sometimes hefty doses of humility and humor (*humorlity*?). But more epic is the fail that involves out-and-out sin. If there's sin, there's only one way to handle it. God's way. We First-John-One-Nine it.

I know. Telling ministers' wives they have to confess and repent. It's a weird and rudimentary thing to do. But how easily we can become lazy in the most basic tenets of the faith—the things we've done a million times. We can become desensitized, thinking that the "repent" thing is for the spiritually immature or those with big-time sins. *O Lord, may our sin always break our hearts. And may we always be quick to fall humbly on our faces in repentance before You.*

Maybe we also need a reminder now and then that the scope of our confession should be equal to the scope of our sin. If we offend one person, we can make it right one-on-one. If we've sinned before the church, then that's exactly how we should seek forgiveness. Very public sin requires equally public confession and repentance.

I'll insert here also the reminder that sweeping sin under the rug is not the way to go. We end up with a compounded problem. Plus a lumpy rug. Proverbs 28:13 (ESV) says, "Whoever conceals his transgressions will not prosper, but he who confesses and forsakes them will obtain mercy." We are freed when we handle our sin God's way. And our people learn by our example what they should do when they fall into sin. In the long run, the Lord can actually use the situation to bless your church.

LET'S HIT THE ROAD

Our Father is always beautifully heavy on the mercy spoken of in that last verse. Whatever our flub, His mercy is there to cover and restore. And to use that mercy to teach us all the more to extend it to others.

The bottom line: we need to get serious about the flubs that are sin. And we need to try to lighten up about everything that isn't, while still keeping a secure hold on our sensitivity toward others (as you'll read in Robin's testimony). And we need to guard against mixing up the two.

Then we need to let His grace and mercy pick us up, dust us off, and move forward in ministry. Hit the road, as it were.

And let me suggest we all check the tops of our cars first.

P-Dub to P-Dub with ROBIN McCALL

At the age of 40, I found myself in the position of learning to be a pastor's wife. Our congregation is a merger of three churches. In addition to being initiated into the pastorate during menopause, I also tiptoed amongst three church cultures melding into one.

Since it's just us girls here, let me confess that I was almost taken down by a piece of cake. Our first baby tea was picture perfect. Fabulous cake, exquisite punch, impeccably sliced ribbon sandwiches, and fruit adorned pristinely polished silver. As our guests arrived, I realized no one was serving cake, so I darted over to the cake table. With my first slice, I looked up to a hushed group of women staring at me like I had grown a third eye.

Why had no one told me that Mrs. Gloria* *always* served cake? After much groveling on my part, Mrs. Gloria accepted her sterling cake knife and retook her rightful position.

In my proud spirit I asked, *How can serving cake become an ordeal? What difference does it make?* After allowing me to wallow in self-righteous indignation, the Lord tugged at my heart. It makes a big difference when another woman's heart is hurt because of my indifference. My little deal was Mrs. Gloria's big deal. What has come to be known as "The Cake Event" was never about cake. It was about extending respect and love and grace, and allowing others to exercise their gifts. You know, that sounds a lot like simply treating others the way our Savior treats us.

*Not her real name

P-DUB PARTNER-LINK: You can find an easy link at rhondarhea.com at the P-Dub tab.

P-DUB POSTSCRIPTS

Passages to Plug In

If we [freely] admit that we have sinned and con-fess our sins, He is faithful and just (true to His own

*nature and promises) and will forgive our sins [dis-
miss our lawlessness] and [continuously] cleanse
us from all unrighteousness [everything not in con-
formity to His will in purpose, thought, and action]*
(1 John 1:9 AMP).

Ponderings to Pose

Robin chose to show respect and extend love and grace in
"The Cake Event." Are there any areas you feel the Lord
might be calling you to rise above? Even more urgent, are
there any areas of sin you haven't dealt with?

My son Andy is a singer/songwriter. He has a song that's
been stuck in my head for several days. It's called "Eden"
and is written from the point of view of the Father to the
fallen Adam. The part that sticks in my head is the very end
of the song when the Father says to His broken Adam, "Look
beyond the edge of you and I'll be there, / There is not a load
for you that I won't bear."

(You can hear the song at http://www.youtube.com
/watch?v=nIeveeTeaVc or find the easy link at rhondarhea
.com. "Eden" from The Corners, words and music by Andy
Rhea, lyric video produced by Joe McGarry.)

Petitions to Pray

Reading 1 John 1:9 in a different version can help keep us
from zipping through it in its familiarity without soaking in
its full meaning. Are there any areas where the Lord might
be tapping on your shoulder about a sin? Ready to First-
John-One-Nine it? Pray through the passage above in the
Amplified Bible version and personalize each part. Then you
can also ask the Lord to:

- Help you distinguish a flub from a sin and respond in the right way to either.
- Help you accept His grace, mercy, and forgiveness and to move on in ministry.
- Turn even the flubs into victory and use it all in the lives of others, for His glory.

CHAPTER 7

Constructing Myself a Pedestal

What does a spiritual giant look like, anyway?
Reminding ourselves exactly what makes us
"spiritual" people.

WHEN I WAS A KID, I always wondered why anyone would ever choose Franken Berry breakfast cereal over Count Chocula. I wondered because . . . chocolate. That was my entire reason. Of course, even though I was only a kid, I still instinctively knew that cereal chocolate didn't really count as true chocolate. It was actually the first bite of Cocoa Krispies that tipped me off. It was more like: snap, crackle, I don't think so.

COUNTERFEITING CHOCOLATE — PRETTY SURE IT'S A FELONY

I've just never been all that cuckoo for Cocoa Puffs. I think it might be simulated. Simulated *what* I don't know. It doesn't smell right. It's like a cross between moldy baby-oiled aluminum and those sweetened paper strips designed to trap ants. Spoiled, oiled, or foiled—I don't know that either.

Calling cereal chocolate real chocolate would be like calling cereal marshmallows real marshmallows. I know it's supposed to be to a breakfast cereal's credit when it stays crunchy even in milk, but I don't think that's supposed to go for the 'mallows. Whenever you bite down on a marshmallow, you shouldn't be able to hear it. Styrofoam-squeaky-hissy noises give me the shivers. Whatever those things are, they're just not right.

They're not marshmallows. It's not chocolate.

Crumble Ho Hos in a bowl. Add milk. *There* is your chocolate cereal.

COUNTERFEITING SPIRITUALITY — THAT LEAVES A BAD TASTE TOO

There's always disappointment in encountering something fake. So much more so when you're talking about fake spirituality. Sometimes we don't even set out to be fake. P-dubs get a super-religiosity label automatically pasted on us by some. Half the time we're not the ones who construct the pedestal. Still, we get into real trouble when we read that label and we try to fake our way into matching it. We get into even bigger trouble when we start to actually believe it.

Hey thanks for this nice pedestal. Could you give me a little boost?

WILL THE REAL SPIRITUAL GIANT PLEASE STAND UP

What is it that makes us "spiritual" people? It's not about who we marry. It's not about any position in any church or ministry. It certainly doesn't happen in setting ourselves above others. Being a Jesus follower is more about climbing down off that pedestal and washing dirty feet.

The scene never ceases to amaze me. "So He got up from supper, laid aside His robe, took a towel, and tied it around Himself. Next, He poured water into a basin and began to wash His disciples' feet and to dry them with the towel tied around Him" (John 13:4–5). The Son of God, our Redeemer, the King of kings, put on a servant's costume and took on the humiliating task of the lowliest servant. And later,

> When Jesus had washed their feet and put on His robe, He reclined again and said to them, "Do you know what I have done for you? You call Me Teacher and Lord. This is well said, for I am. So if I, your Lord and Teacher, have washed your feet, you also ought to wash one another's feet. For I have given you an example that you also should do just as I have done for you" (vv. 12–15).

I wonder if sometimes we feel so compelled to look "spiritual" that we forget to *be* spiritual. Or if we even let ourselves lose touch with what real spirituality is.

FOR SALE. ONE PEDESTAL. ONLY SLIGHTLY USED. WILL ALSO TRADE FOR ALTAR.

Paul said "spiritual" worship is "to present your bodies as a living sacrifice" (Romans 12:1 ESV). Wow. Big difference between a pedestal and an altar of sacrifice. This convicts me. This is about humbling ourselves further than getting off the pedestal, further still than even the foot washing.

The spiritual giant is the one who loves Jesus all the way to the altar of sacrifice. She's the one who allows that love to show up in the most humble service. She's the one who sacrifices every single part of herself and continually allows the Holy Spirit to work out His love in and through her. "Spiritual" is the result of being "Spirit-filled."

And don't you love it that the Lord has tagged a blessing

onto the sacrifice? John 13:17 concludes the foot-washing passage by saying, "If you know these things, you are blessed if you do them."

So let's know and do and be blessed. All out of love for Him. Because . . . Jesus. That's my entire reason.

P-Dub to P-Dub with LORI MOODY

What is a spiritual giant? "For man looks at the outward appearance, but the Lord looks at the heart" (1 Samuel 16:7 NASB).

In our humanness, we cannot fully discern true spirituality or what might constitute a spiritual giant. When one thinks of a spiritual giant, one might think of a woman so brave that she risks her life for others, such as Corrie ten Boom. One thinks of missionaries who have left family and most worldly possessions to love and live with an unreached people group. Some might think of Billy Graham, who has preached to many millions, as a spiritual giant. What about the pastor who preaches faithfully to a small congregation? Might he be a spiritual giant, as well? What about a loving mother or grandmother who wears out her knees praying for her children? While she may not live to see the fruit of her labor, those prayers can change the direction of her family for generations to come.

True spirituality takes time and manifests itself in facing and passing life's tests. The full extent of those tests are known by God, but not necessarily by man. True spirituality possesses a robust vitality which enriches everything it touches. It is precious in the sight of the Lord: "Rather let it be the hidden person of the heart, with the incorruptible beauty of a gentle and quiet spirit, which is very precious in the sight of God" (1 Peter 3:4 NKJV).

P-DUB PARTNER-LINK: http://www.youtube.com
/watch?v=mtKdj9N_pkU

You can find an easy link at rhondarhea.com at the P-Dub tab.

P-DUB POSTSCRIPTS

Passages to Plug In

But he gives more grace. Therefore it says, "God opposes the proud, but gives grace to the humble." Submit yourselves therefore to God. Resist the devil, and he will flee from you. Draw near to God, and he will draw near to you. Cleanse your hands, you sinners, and purify your hearts, you double-minded. Be wretched and mourn and weep. Let your laughter be turned to mourning and your joy to gloom. Humble yourselves before the Lord, and he will exalt you (James 4:6–10 ESV).

Ponderings to Pose

Lori Moody begins with 1 Samuel 16:7. What are some ways others tend to look on the outward appearance to determine how spiritual a person is? What are some ways we do? Can you think of other passages that remind us what kind of "heart" the Lord is looking for?

Petitions to Pray

Ask the Lord to align your thinking about what makes us spiritual with His thinking. Spend some time in prayer humbling yourself before Him, James 4:10 style. Then let the Lord exalt you, not in any kind of counterfeit way, but in His genuinely love-filled way, all because of the borrowed righteousness of Christ.

CHAPTER 8

Don't Go Down with the Friend Ship: Keeping Friendships Afloat

Is it normal to feel lonely when we're surrounded by so many people? Looking at what to do with that loneliness and taking a close look at close friends.

ANYTIME YOU TRIP IN FRONT of your friends, the best thing to do is just to bounce right back up and keep on going. To the airport. And then leave the country. Maybe change your name.

Isn't it a little hard to save face after your face just did a plant? Especially a face plant on gravel. Exfoliation gone so wrong.

The last time I took a tumble I didn't do a face plant, so there was no eating gravel or anything. But I think I do remember the faint taste of linoleum for a while. It was in a busy hallway at church. So it was really more the taste of linoleum *and humiliation*. That'll leave a mark. I'm thinking it could be the kind of mark that requires some industrial-strength concealer.

It's always nice to have friends nearby who will help you up. Well actually, to laugh uproariously for several minutes first and then make merciless fun of you for years. But at least they do help you up somewhere in between.

THE IMPACT OF FRIENDS

Would it surprise you to learn that the number one problem pastors' wives report regarding life in the ministry is loneliness? *Numero uno.* Surrounded by people, yet still feeling isolated. Has it happened to you? Now at least you know you're not the only one. And all too often a p-dub gets hurt in a friendship and vows never to try it again. More isolation. More loneliness. More frustration, heartache—even depression.

We were created with a need for connection. It's in our blueprints. You need a girlfriend. And while it's true that this book is designed with connection in mind, you need more than a book and some videos. This is a great place to start and a sweet place for camaraderie, relatability, some laughs, and some practical helps. But you need more. You need more than your Facebook friends too. You need a flesh-and-blood, have-coffee-with-you, call-you-for-no-reason, hold-you-account-able, go-shopping-with-you, let-you-crab-about-how-much-weight-you've-gained, laugh-with-you, cry-with-you, real-live girlfriend. We simply can't get away from the truth that we were designed by our Creator with that need deeply imbed-ded into our makeup—and no, by "makeup" I'm not really talking "concealer."

Don't conceal or ignore that connection need. While all of us will experience times in life when close friendships are fewer and farther between, we need to do everything we can to make those seasons short. Sometimes that means we have to make the first move. Make the effort. Sometimes it means we have to learn to trust again even after we've been hurt. Take the risk.

I love the reminder in Ecclesiastes 4:9–10: "Two are better than one because they have a good reward for their efforts. For if either falls, his companion can lift him up; but pity the one who falls without another to lift him up." You never know when you're going to need a pick-me-up. Find yourself a bud.

Proverbs 18:24 (ESV) also makes a thought-provoking point. "A man of many companions may come to ruin, but there is a friend who sticks closer than a brother." There are times when it's not enough to simply have someone standing by. Those surfacey kinds of acquaintances will come and go in our lives. But there is a true and lasting blessing in a friend who's with you through all your ups and downs. Through every victory and through every tumble. And there's great blessing in becoming that kind of friend to someone as well.

FRIENDS ARE GREAT IN A SCRAPE

In all the varied happenings of p-dub life, we need each other—whether we've just taken a header or sometimes just as much when we're gracefully tiptoeing along. I find myself remembering all the more clearly each time a close friend offers godly counsel or encourages me to seek the Lord. I remember it well each time friends spur me on or inspire me to walk closer to Christ by their godly example. And yes, still again each time a friend helps scrape me off the pavement after a spill.

If you're experiencing one of those seasons in life when a close friend is not as accessible, could I encourage you to keep praying, asking the Lord to send a bud your way? Who knows? He might drop one right in front of you. Maybe even in a church hallway. On linoleum.

63

Meanwhile, Psalm 37:23–24 (NIV) tells us, "The LORD makes firm the steps of the one who delights in him; though he may stumble, he will not fall, for the Lord upholds him with his hand." Whether there is a friend nearby or you're waiting for one, the Lord is never absent or inattentive. Even if there's a bit of a spill, we're lovingly held.

True friends? They're a blessed bonus. It's amazing how the Lord can use them to impact our lives for Him.

Good impact. Because now we know there's impact, and there's impact on linoleum.

P-Dub to P-Dub with CYNTHIA HOPKINS

When my husband and I were just starting out in ministry, a p-dub told me that she would never form a close friendship with another church member again. She had done that once, and had been burned. I felt sad for her, and decided then and there that I didn't ever want to feel that way.

Years later, though, I was the one getting burned. It wasn't a superclose friend, but close enough for it to make me understand what that p-dub had felt years before. And it stinks!

I've been a p-dub now for 23 years. I have seen and felt enough to know that you do have to do things differently. At the same time, I think that maybe the problem that p-dubs see is just a really sharp picture of the problem in most female friendships. P-dubs can't tell all, complain to their church friends about church stuff, or spend all their time with one or two friends. Neither should non p-dubs. When it comes to obedience to God's commands and following His purposes in the world, every believer is called to the same standard.

So, yeah, I've been burned before, but I still don't want to shy away from friendship. I don't think that's what God wants, either. What He wants is for me to obey Him in those relationships, and to keep His purposes as my priority.

P-DUB PARTNER-LINK: http://www.youtube.com /watch?v=a0EsUqgAKXY

You can find an easy link at rhondarhea.com at the P-Dub tab.

P-DUB POSTSCRIPTS

Passages to Plug In

Two people are better off than one, for they can help each other succeed. If one person falls, the other can reach out and help. But someone who falls alone is in real trouble. Likewise, two people lying close together can keep each other warm. But how can one be warm alone? A person standing alone can be attacked and defeated, but two can stand back-to-back and conquer. Three are even better, for a triple-braided cord is not easily broken (Ecclesiastes 4:9–12 NLT).

Ponderings to Pose

Cynthia Hopkins mentions that as ministers' wives, we have to do some aspects of friendship a little differently. There are times we can't share everything or we might betray a confidence. How can you find the balance between being able to share your heart and sharing too much information?

Petitions to Pray

Pick an if or two to pray.

- If you're experiencing smothering loneliness, ask the Lord to send you a "breath-of-fresh-air" kind of friend. Ask Him to help you become someone else's breath of fresh air as well.

- If you've been wounded in a friendship, ask the Lord to give you the ability to forgive and to help you move forward and trust again.
- If you're not already, ask the Lord to give you the courage to become proactive in making and maintaining friendships.
- If you have at least one close friend, thank the Lord for the amazing blessing she is. Ask Him to make you a blessing to her and to give each of you wisdom in honoring Him through the friendship.

CHAPTER 9

Leftovers, Again?

When your husband is meeting the urgent need du jour at church, it can feel as if the church gets first dibs on him and the wife gets whatever's left. How do we deal?

SOMETIMES THE STRUGGLE IN THE kitchen for me is more than just the challenge of not being all that adept at cooking. Though, let's get real, that's no small challenge. But it's also frustrating that the second I try to think of something to put together to make a meal, I feel every ounce of creativity drain out of my being.

One afternoon, I opened the fridge door and the ketchup bottle fell out and exploded. So I did the only sensible thing. Drew a chalk outline around it and left to get pizza—because that seems like what you should serve when you're hosting a murder mystery party.

That would've been the most creative thing I'd ever done in the kitchen, except that I just made it all up. Do I at least get creative points for that?

A DINNER CRIME AND A CONFESSION

Here's another confession: sometimes I have cereal for dinner. Even though it's essentially the "I give up" of domestic and culinary achievement. I told my family a few nights ago that I could make them absolutely anything for dinner they wanted. As long as they wanted canned soup and grilled cheese.

When I finally do come up with a dinner idea that's halfway interesting, it's sad that it so often takes an evil turn. I tried a meat casserole-type thing one time. Let me just call it what it was—it was a log of meat. The family didn't eat much of it, surprise, surprise. No tip for me that night. But how many days can you serve the same leftovers? What was most fascinating was that every time I warmed it up for another go-round, it looked different than it did the day before. Morph-meat-loaf. Creepiest leftovers ever.

GETTING THE BEST OF HIM

When it comes to your husband's leftover time, it can be even tougher to deal with the feeling that everyone at church is getting the creative and fresh part of him. He's logging in extra hours (yeah, different kind of log) and you start to feel you're sort of getting the table scraps.

The majority of churches in America have less than 200 people. That usually means small staff—often a staff of one. Is that your hubs? That means he's always on call as the pastor, the accountant, the counselor, the wedding and funeral officiator, the one who sets up the chairs and cranks up the furnace, the one who plans the events, and the one who does most of the work in carrying them out. He's the tech guy, the resident answerer of all things spiritual, and also the guy people call when there's a plumbing leak in the church basement. The poor man gets tugged from every direction. There are generally about as many tugs for support staff, evangelists, denominational ministers, missionaries—all our pastor/husbands.

Then there are those people who don't respect his time —or your time with him—and expect him to drop everything to be at their beck and call. Balancing being available and guarding family time can be a tough call for any minister.

Sometimes our husbands really are too busy for too long, and we need to honestly, yet with a heaping helping of grace, let them know we're feeling a little too far down on the list of priorities. There may be some things he can rearrange or others he can delegate. Some seasons in his ministry, though, are busier than others, and there are times we simply need to ask the Lord to help us patiently wait it out. Mostly the "patiently" part is about asking the Lord to make us gracious when he doesn't have a moment to spare, and to ask Him to be the one to change our husbands' schedule. The other part of "patiently" is getting through it all without trying to whine, nag, guilt or otherwise manipulate the changes ourselves. Building up, not tearing down. "Every wise woman builds her house, but a foolish one tears it down with her own hands" (Proverbs 14:1).

Men in ministry need that building up. Encouraging them is a huge part of our own ministry. First Thessalonians 5:11 (ESV) isn't only for pastors' families, but it surely does apply: "Therefore encourage one another and build one another up, just as you are doing" (ESV).

TIP THE BALANCE

Chances are your husband is already struggling to juggle the stress—the guilt from being so often away from home, plus the extra stresses of dealing with people and their "stuff." It really is a tough balance between showing understanding and patience while still letting our husbands know we need some honey-time. I'll confess (what, another confession?)— I don't always get the balance.

When a family calls with an urgent crisis and needs my husband, there've been a few times I wanted to grab the phone and interrupt with, "Excuse me, but could you possibly reschedule your grandfather's passing for another night? I made soup and grilled cheese here."

There are things that take him away from home— sometimes at freaky or incredibly inconvenient hours— things that he simply can't reschedule. It's those times we have to lean hard into Jesus, asking Him to help us guard against manipulating and further guilting our husbands. And we need to ask Him to help us never, ever see the church as our competition. His ministry? It's our ministry too. And we need to have our hearts fully in it. Only Jesus can keep them there.

HEATING UP

Once it becomes all about what we're giving up, we lose sight of the ministry. We need to be constantly asking the Lord to fire up our hearts to see changed lives—asking Him to keep fresh our straining and yearning to see the hearts of people turn to Him—to let us see ministry making a difference because of what He's doing through our husbands. It's got to be about what Jesus is doing, or we'll be right back around to whining and manipulating. Hearts freshly on fire. No warmed up leftovers will do. They're just creepy.

When it's all about what the Lord wants to do in the lives of people, then encouraging and comforting and helping our husbands in all their busyness happens a whole lot more easily.

I'd say as easy as falling off a log, but we're really not over that yet. Still just too soon.

P-Dub to P-Dub with BETSY BARTIG

Early on in our ministry, a dear elderly man, Mr. Jackson, was brave enough to mentor us as a young couple fresh in the ministry. In one mentoring session about communication, he said, "There are two ways to tell a woman she's ugly. 'Honey, your face can stop a clock!' Or, 'You have a face that makes time stand still.'"

I know we all experience times in our marriage when ministry seems to rule over our husband's time and we get the "leftovers." When that happens to me, I remember from Mr. Jackson that I have two choices in how I communicate. I can pout, whine, or give him the silent treatment. (Let's face it, we've tried those.) Or I can wait for his free moments. I can take the time to say "I love you," touch his hand and look into his eyes, and let him know I'm covering him in prayer as he walks out the door to another busy day.

Ministry will always demand our husband's time, but God has always been faithful to provide us with seasons of rest. I encourage you to enjoy the time you have together—no matter how long or short. You've only been given "today" with your husband. "But encourage one another daily, as long as it is called Today" (Hebrews 3:13 NIV).

P-DUB PARTNER-LINK: http://www.youtube.com /watch?v=yHJw2PHEOKQ

You can find an easy link at rhondarhea.com at the P-Dub tab.

P-DUB POSTSCRIPTS

Passages to Plug In

So let us seize and hold fast and retain without wavering the hope we cherish and confess and our acknowledgement of it, for He Who promised is reliable (sure) and faithful to His word. And let us consider and give attentive, continuous care to watching over one another, studying how we may stir up (stimulate and incite) to love and helpful deeds and noble activities, Not forsaking or neglecting to assemble together [as believers], as is the habit of some people, but admonishing (warning, urging, and encouraging) one another, and all the more faithfully as you see the day approaching (Hebrews 10:23–25 AMP).

Ponderings to Pose

Betsy Bartig encourages us to encourage. Do you know what encourages your husband in particular? The "Passage to Plug In" in Hebrews says to "give attentive, continuous care to watching over one another, studying how we may stir up" ministry. Finding out what encourages your husband might be a lifelong study. But the homework pays off.

Petitions to Pray

Ask the Lord to give you wisdom, patience, and grace for those seasons when the demands of your husband's ministry leave a smaller amount of time for you. Just a couple of extra prayer points:

- Help me show patience at the right time.
- Help me to know when to encourage him to slow down and when to just plain encourage him.

- Lord, show me just what will encourage my husband and give me the strength and selflessness to do it.

CHAPTER 10

The Perfect P-Dub Grub

Real spiritual food for real women—everything we truly need for victorious, successful p-dubbing.

MY KIDS ARE ALL IN their early 20s and all very tech-savvy, so it was really funny the other day when they saw one of the earliest cell phones. I'm talking vintage here—just this side of fossilized. And huge. A dinosaur in every way. I dubbed it "Cell-a-saurus Rex." My kids thought it must be some sort of coffee grinder. I think one of them was trying to get it to churn butter.

If you want to know what it was really like with those first mobile phones, try holding your microwave oven up to your ear. All the mobile phone bells and whistles? I'm pretty sure on those first phones, they were actual bells and whistles. I told my kids that I thought people probably had a tough time, back then, knowing if a guy was listening to his boom box or talking on his cell phone. Of course, then I had to explain what a boom box was. I told them it was like a giant MP3 player. I'm thankful technology is always evolving, coming up with something bigger and better. Or sometimes something smaller and better.

SUPERSIZING OUR FAITH

I want a big faith. I really do. I want supersized faith with all the bells and whistles. But sometimes size is pretty relative. When the disciples asked Jesus to give them bigger faith, Jesus answered in a rather surprising way. In Luke 17:5–6 the disciples said to Jesus,

> *"Increase our faith." Jesus' answer? "If you have faith the size of a mustard seed, you can say to this mulberry tree, 'Be uprooted and planted in the sea,' and it will obey you."*

Matthew 17:20 (ESV) tells us that Jesus said,

> *For truly, I say to you, if you have faith like a grainof mustard seed, you will say to this mountain, "Move from here to there," and it will move, and nothing will be impossible for you* (Matthew 17:20 ESV).

According to Jesus Himself, with even the tiniest faith, we can do huge things. Impossible things. Impossible things like bearing fruit in our ministries. Even finding great joy in it. It's not so much the *size* of the faith as it is *whom* the faith trusts. A faith planted firmly in Christ and an obedient response to His lordship makes a huge impact on life. Mountainous!

FAITH — ON THE CELLULAR LEVEL

It's good to remember that faith grows at the deepest part of who we are. At the "cellular" level, if you will. Not just the p-dub, surface parts. Not even just the p-dub service parts. But all the way to the heart.

Paul tells us in Romans 10:17 that faith comes by hearing and hearing by the Word of God. Don't you love it that His Word teaches us about His character, His history, His power, and His incomparable trustworthiness? Studying the character of God has changed my faith. It always changes our faith—all the way down to our deepest, heart-of-heart parts. The more we study Him through His Word, and the more we know Him, the more we respond in obedience, and the more our faith grows.

I want to be a good example of a strong faith before the people we minister to, sure. But I also want big faith because I love and trust the Savior. And that's what He wants.

CAN YOU HEAR ME NOW?

Jesus said in Luke 8:18, "Therefore take care how you listen. For whoever has, more will be given to him; and whoever does not have, even what he thinks he has will be taken away from him."

We never come to a place in this life where we've had enough of God's Word. Never. And according to this verse, there's a bonus! When you hear God's Word and believe it, you get more of it. Want to be equipped to minister and to lead out? It takes more understanding, more faith, more Him through His Word. Likewise, when we hear God's Word without faith to receive it, we get less. Less understanding, less fruit—just plain less. Hebrews 4:2 says, "For good news came to us just as to them, but the message they heard did not benefit them, because they were not united by faith with those who listened" (ESV). The kind of hearing the Lord wants us to have is the kind that is securely tied to faith. If we hear what God says in His Word, but don't believe it or act on it, it's just like we never heard it.

A HEARING FAITH

We see the topic come up again in Hebrews 5:11 when Scripture says, "About this we have much to say, and it is hard to explain, since you have become dull of hearing" (ESV). What is it these people are not getting? More Jesus. More understanding of who He is and why their faith is completely safe when it's placed in Him. More understanding of why they should live for Him no matter what. More understanding of life itself. The next verses tell us,

> *For though by this time you ought to be teachers, you need someone to teach you again the basic principles of the oracles of God. You need milk, not solid food, for everyone who lives on milk is unskilled in the word of righteousness, since he is a child. But solid food is for the mature, for those who have their powers of discernment trained by constant practice to distinguish good from evil* (vv. 12–14 ESV).

Milk's not the p-dub grub for us! We need to be done with the baby food. We won't survive this p-dub life in any kind of victory without the solid food we find in the Bible. Any time we let time invested in the Word slide, we're making a baby move. Sometimes we even read all over it—grabbing a bit here and a bit there for that Bible study we're teaching or something clever for that class we're leading. I don't know about you, but I don't want to be just "over" the Word of God. I want to be in it. Really in. It's got to be personal. Our call is to build our faith by being completely committed to His Word. This may be the most important call we get all day. Yep. In every way. A personal call.

P-Dub to P-Dub with ROBIN BRYCE

Within the first seven years of ministry, my marriage hit the rocks. The demands of the church had been more important than family and marriage. Hurt tremendously, I thought of divorce, murder, and even suicide. [The Book of] Hosea and I became tight, since we both loved spouses whose attention went elsewhere. Try being mad at the church! Eventually, we overcame with godly counseling and prayer. That's when I found God was all I needed, and I learned to breathe freely.

Breathe in the Word of the Lord; breathe out a changed life unto the Lord. This isn't another Bible study. Rather, it begins with a request, "God, reveal yourself to me today." Then we read the Bible listening for God to speak to us personally. When he does, obey and breathe out a changed life.

Breathe in a conversation with the Lord; breathe out the faith, hope, and love of the Lord. This is talking with God about what He said earlier. I find He continues to speak as I write my prayer to Him, and he often prompts me to action: to breathe out faith, hope, and love.

Breathe in the presence of the Lord; breathe out the essence of the Lord. When remaining in God's presence becomes our strongest desire, our time spent with Him changes the time spent with others. We become the Ambassadors of God.

To be spiritually fed, we only have sincerely to breathe in these things. As we do, God supernaturally takes care of the breathing out.

P-DUB PARTNER-LINK: http://youtu.be/ELW9AbG0iq0

You can find an easy link at rhondarhea.com at the P-Dub tab.

P-DUB POSTSCRIPTS

Passages to Plug In

Unless Your law had been my delight, I would have perished in my affliction. I will never forget Your precepts, [how can I?] *for it is by them You have quickened me (granted me life). . . . I have seen that everything* [human] *has its limits and end* [no matter how extensive, noble, and excellent]; *but Your commandment is exceedingly broad and extends without limits* [into eternity] (Psalm 119:92–93, 96 AMP).

Ponderings to Pose

What would happen if we didn't make the time to breathe? I know, right? Robin Bryce gives us a beautiful picture of communion with the Father as our breath. Are there any ways you can strengthen your spiritual breathing that come to mind? Are you ready to continue in or formulate your own personal "breathing" plan?

Petitions to Pray

The psalms give us great fuel for prayer. Use this paraphrase of Psalm 119:129–136 for your prayer points:

> *Every word you give me is a miracle word—*
>   *how could I help but obey?*
> *Break open your words, let the light shine out,*
>   *let ordinary people see the meaning.*
> *Mouth open and panting,*
>   *I wanted your commands more than anything*
> (Psalm 119:129–36 *The Message*)

CHAPTER 11

Lovin' the Hub in the P-Dub Club

There's joy in loving our husbands well. Remembering that we're the only ones who can let our pastor feel he's a successful husband. Guarding our marriages.

IT'S SO FUNNY. I WENT into my office to get something the other day, but when I got there, I couldn't remember what it was. So I wrote a book. Still, I don't see how this brain can be firing on all cylinders when I can walk into—hold on, where was I walking again? To top it off, I was leaving town not long after that to work on another book with my daughter, and halfway through the four-hour journey, I suddenly had that panicked feeling. *Oh no! I left the stove on!* Then I thought, *Wait. I never use the stove.* So I had a good laugh that lasted for a solid 75 miles.

With or without the forgetfulness, it can be slowgoing on these book projects. And it's not that I mind hard work. I don't. It's just that mostly I would rather other people do it.

WHAT DID I COME IN HERE FOR?

OK, on the whole, that's a joke. I do know that the Bible

says that working with the right kind of heart attitude means I work just like I'm working for Jesus. Because I *am* working for Jesus. "Serve wholeheartedly, as if you were serving the Lord, not people" (Ephesians 6:7 NIV). That truth makes all the difference in the world. Because you know what? I need to remember what I'm here for. Remembering why I'm here helps me also remember to trade my time for something kingdom-redeemable.

Our marriages. They're rightly and tightly included in that kingdom-redeemable category. Every bit of work and time invested there is well spent. There may be a lot of things I forget, but I want to always remember "what I came into this marriage for."

ONENESS OR WITHOUT-NESS

Marriage is about oneness. We're to show off the loving character of God—display His oneness with His church—through our marriages. We can't go rogue and try to accomplish this outside His plan or without His strength to make it happen and expect any kind of success. Without oneness we're without success.

Let's roll up our sleeves, sisters, and get ready to work, honoring our marriages and honoring our husbands. We need to work with our full-on energies to nurture and protect our relationships, our husbands, and their successes. Building up. Never tearing down. We looked at Proverbs 14:1 a couple of chapters back. "Every wise woman builds her house, but a foolish one tears it down with her own hands." (Proverbs 14:1). The building of the house here refers to increasing its wealth, value, success, or influence. At every place we're building our husbands' influence, supporting them in the role God called them to, we're walking in wisdom. There's joy there.

WORK ON MARRIAGE IN THE WISE DIRECTION

I counseled a pastor's wife a few months ago, who came to me because she was struggling in her marriage. She was frustrated with her husband's depression and anger. But she didn't only confide in me, she also went to their closest friends at church—a married couple, both in leadership. Then a handful of other church members. I think she thought she was working on her marriage, but I probably don't need to tell you that she essentially imploded her husband's effectiveness at that church. She devalued his success and influence, tearing it down in the exact fashion of the negative, foolish opposite of Proverbs 14:1.

Not only were her actions calamitous for her husband's ministry, but it's so sad that this woman sabotaged the oneness of her marriage at the same time. Her husband was embarrassed, pretty humiliated actually, held up as a public failure in his marriage. It's not only going to be tough to recover at church, but rebuilding trust in marriage and forgiving a perceived betrayal are all now added to the struggles he was already experiencing.

Getting counseling can be a very wise move. But we have to take extra care that we get it from the right person, in the right way, at the right place. Going behind a husband's back and sharing private marriage issues willy-nilly is never the wise move. There are no doubt Christian counselors not associated with your church or area of ministry who could offer some practical help and perspective. Be wise. Be loyal.

WORK STUDY

Everyone has shortcomings, your hubby included. But let's make it a goal that not a single person will ever hear about those shortcomings from us. Be his advocate. Be his PR gal.

You really are the only one who can make your man feel like a successful husband. The only one. That's a lot of power to wield. We also looked at Hebrews 10:24 in chapter 9. The Amplified Bible version says to "give attentive, continuous care to watching over one another, studying how we may stir up" ministry. There's wisdom in becoming a student of how to encourage this man and to comfort and inspire him in ministry. This is Husband 101—and we all need to be perpetually enrolled in the class. Back to school!

It's wonderfully healthy for your marriage when you invest time and effort in finding out what his dreams are. Tell him yours too. Spend time together as much as you can, in and outside ministry. Laugh together. Those are healthy ways we can work to guard our relationship. Could I prompt you as well to talk about him behind his back? But in a good way. Talk about his strengths and gifts to others—when he's not around and just as much when he is. There aren't a lot of things in this world that will hearten him more.

HEAD CHEERLEADER AT THE SCHOOL OF HUB-STUDY

Let me encourage you to do everything you can to convince your husband that you're his biggest fan. I *am* my husband's biggest fan. This man has so much to cheer about it's hard to know where to begin the *siss-* and where to end the *boom-bah*. But my adoration of all things Richie doesn't do much for him if I don't let him know—convince him—it's true.

Incidentally, if you're not feeling those loving feelings for him as strongly as you once did, remind yourself of that long list of attributes that attracted you to him in the beginning of your relationship. It may be hypocritical for me to talk about "remembering" anything, but still. *These things* I remember.

Then love him by faith. Ask the Lord to do a rekindling. It's His will for you and for your marriage. When we pray according to His will, He hears. And He *does*. You'll be amazed at what your Father will do!

BRING ON THE ONENESS!

Let's keep on remembering to work for oneness, doing whatever it takes. Never underestimate, for example, the fact that investing in extraordinary prayer for your husband is mind-blowingly powerful. You can do other things too. Like trying to get away to a marriage conference or retreat now and then—where neither one of you is leading or teaching. You can be accountable—and guard yourself against any situation where you're in danger of giving yourself emotionally to another, even a little. More and more women—even ministers' wives—are getting fooled into heading in a devastating, destructive direction. By the way, Richie and I have complete access to each other's email and any social media communication. The door to his office has a nice, big pane of glass in it. Accountability is good for all of us.

Most of all, everything will fall into place as we keep loving Jesus at the center of our marriages. Is it possible to be a minister and a minister's wife and not have a Christ-centered marriage? Yes. Yet we should devote ourselves to keep Christ at the center. He's the One we came in for!

P-Dub to P-Dub with *JOYCE DINKINS*

If a truck ran over Steven, my husband, he would get up, dust off, and say, "Praise the Lord!" That's why God made us care for each other—this month we're celebrating 25 years loving—since I've taken some heavy life hits too. We are a perfect pair of *broken folks*. Broken by illness, financial loss, loved ones' deaths . . . and the life list goes on, as it does for humans.

Brokenness made me and Steven pliable for God's motherly molding. So we've fallen deeply in love with our Maker, Savior, and Comforter, then sharing His nurture with others—our family, the churches and senior pastors where Steven has served alongside, and with other broken folks.

Sometimes, we find ourselves "run over" in the process of being Christian, you know? But difficult seasons and incidents prove to us that we're God-tested tough, strong yet tender to His Spirit, Word, prayer. Tender toward widows, orphans, the homeless, the prisoner, the sick.

I thank God for a mutually encouraging mate, for all the years of praising God and rising to serve. And I rejoice in reminding Steven of all that life has brought that would have wrecked us—like what tries to wreck us all—but for God, who always gets us up to stand and dusts us off. Praise Him!

P-DUB PARTNER-LINK:

You can find an easy link at rhondarhea.com at the P-Dub tab.

P-DUB POSTSCRIPTS

Passages to Plug In

Love is patient and kind; love does not envy or boast; it is not arrogant or rude. It does not insist on its own way; it is not irritable or resentful; it does not rejoice at wrongdoing, but rejoices with the truth. Love bears all things, believes all things, hopes all things, endures all things. Love never ends (1 Corinthians 13:4–8 ESV).

Ponderings to Pose

Joyce Dinkins gave us a tender testimony of how the Lord used brokenness. Blind leading the blind? Nothing good happens there. But the broken leading the broken—that's powerful. Lives are changed. We're all broken in some way or another. Have you thought about your own areas of brokenness lately? What are they? How might the Lord use those? How might He use your husband's brokenness? Joyce spoke of her "mutually encouraging" husband. What are some practical ways a couple can become mutually encouraging?

Petitions to Pray

First Corinthians 13 in the Passages to Plug In gives us the perfect prayer points for loving God's way. Lord, help me to show my husband:

- Patience
- Kindness
- Humility
- Unselfishness
- Respect
- Courtesy
- Thoughtfulness
- Fairness
- Honesty
- Forgiveness
- Loyalty
- Commitment

CHAPTER 12

When Papa Ain't Happy

What are we supposed to do when our husband is suffering? Coming alongside your husband in his pain.

SOMEBODY ASKED ME ABOUT a carburetor the other day. I had to remind him that I don't really know much about sports. I know some of you don't think like I do at all on these things. This is to your credit. But in my mind there are several things that shall always remain in the guy category. Sports, tools, killing spiders, working on anything involving electricity, everything under the hood of the car—all on the man list.

Just so you know, though, I can name several parts of my car. Steering wheel, key, visor/vanity mirror, tires, GPS . . . um . . . OK, that's about it. But I do know where to put the key and which direction to turn it—and because my husband is an extremely good sport I haven't needed to know much more than that.

I got a call from our insurance guy the other day and he was asking about the make and model of my car. All I could tell him was, "Well, it's tan. Sort of a beige really. I would describe it as somewhere near the color of cream soda."

And that's when our rates went up.

NOW THAT'S A GOOD SPORT

My husband really is a good sport about everything I've put in the man category, even though it's probably not always convenient for him. Not to mention, there's a sort of pastor category added to that. I think most pastors have too many things that their church folks put in their pastor category, which causes it to become inconvenient and heavy.

I remember reading a few years ago that 70 percent of pastors are in a constant battle with depression. Many researchers point to this statistic. I found that positively staggering. And a little scary. I don't think that even took into consideration those teetering on the edge of it. I sincerely doubt that number has gotten better. With the strange schedules and late nights, the grab-something-on-the-go eating habits, and especially the overwhelming heaviness of the issues of the people he encounters in a day—being overloaded, overstressed, and often underappreciated, it's easy to see how that can happen—though I'm still taken aback by the fact that it happens to the overwhelming majority.

Since those feelings of desperation and defeat crop up so regularly in men in ministry, it's good when we wives can be prepared enough that we're not completely caught off guard by it and can have a few thoughts about ways we might help.

WHAT CAN WE DO?

First, it's good to set our husbands free to share with us about how they're really feeling—even if it doesn't sounds very "spiritual." He needs to be able to speak his mind about feeling depressed and hopeless without his wife expressing judgment. Because of the stigma of the blues, he's more inclined to suffer in silence or feel guilty about feeling disconnected and not being able to simply shake off the sadness. We need to do our best to convince our husbands we want to come alongside them in their struggle and that we're offering a nonjudgmental ear.

We're often our husband's sounding board about a lot of things. And we can get a little too comfortable in the role of devil's advocate. Especially when our husband is struggling with depression or is on the brink of it, the devil doesn't need any more help. We need to be our husband's advocate, not the devil's. Encouraging him to unburden himself can be a big relief and a great comfort to him. The physical has a great bearing on the mental, spiritual, and emotional parts of who we are. It's no quick fix, but encouraging him to get some sunshine, exercise when possible, and to eat a balanced diet can sometimes have an influence on his struggle. If your husband has been depressed for two weeks or more, it's a good idea to give him the nudge to check in with his doctor. Meanwhile, be careful not to get caught up in pessimism or stuck under the dark cloud of depression yourself. You can be the one who cheers and gives hope if he'll let you, and who points your husband to the Hope Giver. Stay optimistic.

THE PLACE OF HOPE

Even in the midst of dark times, our hope is secure when we place it in our loving God. "Why, my soul, are you downcast? Why so disturbed within me? Put your hope in God, for I will yet praise him, my Savior and my God" (Psalm 42:11 NIV). The psalmist had to have little chats with his own soul to remind him where to put his hope. Our hope is just as secure there today as it was for him then.

In those dark times, Psalm 34:18–19 becomes more than a platitude. It's anchoring when we truly take it to heart. "The Lord is near to the brokenhearted and saves the crushed in spirit. Many are the afflictions of the righteous, but the Lord delivers him out of them all" (ESV).

Hang on to the Word of God. Hang on to it for the both of you when you need to. Let the Lord be your secure place. "You are my hiding place and my shield; I hope in your word. . . . Uphold me according to your promise, that I may live, and let me not be put to shame in my hope! Hold me up, that I may be safe and have regard for your statutes continually!" (Psalm 119:114, 116–17 ESV).

Every once in a while, you can jump-start your husband's hope with your own hope. And while I may not know how a jump-start relates to my car—or sports either—I do know His hope is life-saving. Of this I'm very sure.

P-Dub to P-Dub with JANET MCGLAUGHLIN

I've noticed that when Papa ain't happy, I ain't happy. And the kids ain't happy. No one is happy at home, and eventually the church ain't happy, and we have a whole new set of problems.

But there are things we can do. Take a look around you and be thankful. God has a special calling on your husband's life which puts him in the spotlight, causes him to work unusual hours, stand with troubled, sick, and grieving people in their hours of need and strive to point them to God's plans and to encourage them.

So who encourages him? God often works through you. You, too, are called to do whatever it takes to help him be prepared to do his work. You can't really change the circum-stances or fix the problems, but you can bravely walk with him through them, and know that God is controlling them. Sometimes you have the sensitivity to see and hear things he doesn't notice and he needs that input. You are the helpmeet and unwavering cheerleader to him. You can do that part and still have a world of opportunities all your own.

P-DUB PARTNER-LINK: You can find an easy link at rhondarhea.com at the P-Dub tab.

P-DUB POSTSCRIPTS

Passages to Plug In

I waited patiently for the Lord, and He turned to me and heard my cry for help. He brought me up from a desolate pit, out of the muddy clay, and set my feet on a rock, making my steps secure. He put a new song in my mouth, a hymn of praise to our God. Many will see and fear and put their trust in the Lord (Psalm 40:1–3).

Ponderings to Pose

I'm sure the Psalm 40 passage in the Passages to Plug In is a familiar one to you. Don't you love it that after the mud pit comes the rock, and after the rock comes a song of praise, and after that song of praise, there comes a testimony! It's a testimony that makes a difference in the lives of others. Have you seen others who have gone from mud pit to testimony? How does that encourage you, no matter on which side of the pit you or your husband might be?

Petitions to Pray

If we haven't already, each of us needs to develop and maintain active prayer support for our husbands. They need our prayers. Really need them. We touched on it in the last chapter, but we need to know beyond doubt how very vital it is that we be the ones making that spiritual investment. Ask the Lord to give you a practical, daily plan for praying for your husband. Would you be willing to jump-start that plan (or continue yours) right now on your knees?

CHAPTER 13

His and Hers Matching Burnout

One of the number one distresses of pastors and their spouses: burnout. Let's talk about burning UP and not out.

I MAY LOOK CALM ON the outside. But on the inside I'm frantically trying to digest ridiculous amounts of complex carbs without storing any more cellulite. Time to up the metabolism, I'm thinking. Seems the logical fix would be coffee. That's why I figure I'm helping things along if I drive through and pick myself up a grande mocha latte with extra whip.

Someone told me that the average person drinks 22 gallons of coffee a year. I've also heard it said that the average person walks about 8,000 miles a year just going about the regular routine of everyday life. That's got to work off at least the extra whip, wouldn't you think? I'm not one to try out the math, but still, it looks to me like we're getting about 363 miles to the gallon. Talk about sustainability! Suddenly that four-dollar mocha is a responsible purchase, right?

BURN UP, NOT OUT

Burning carbs is one thing. But burning out is another. In the busyness and stresses of going about the not-always-so-regular routine of kingdom work, it's easy to become not just overwhipped, but overworked, overtired and overwhelmed.

Some of the warning signs of burnout? A soul-weariness—a tiredness that rarely goes away. There's also that "spinning your wheels" frustration, feeling that even though you're running yourself ragged, you're not really making a difference. Resentment builds and starts to replace the joy you once found in working for Jesus. It's difficult to love Him well and even harder to love His people. You find yourself fighting against a strong desire to isolate yourself. Loneliness, negativity, cynicism, and hopelessness start to creep in.

What do we do when we feel "whipped"—in the not-creamy-and-delicious way? First, we look *up*. We run to the only One who can heal a heart and refresh a spirit. Nothing new. We do the things that are the most comfortably, reassuringly familiar. If there's sin in the way, we get rid of it. Spending time on our faces in prayer, getting truly honest with the Father, starts the process of reinvigorating an exhausted heart. We immerse ourselves in His word. It's there we find direction, strength, wisdom, and restoration. We determine we're going to stay plugged into people, and we find a godly confidante. We've already discussed the fact that we were designed with the deep need for that people-connection. It's vital.

ALL BURNED OUT AND TOO MANY PLACES TO GO

It's also good to take a look at the schedule and get rid of clutter everywhere we can. The truth is God never calls us to do anything He won't equip us to do. In essence, He won't give you more miles to walk than He gives coffee to get you there. If there's more on the schedule than we have the time and energy to accomplish, that means we've added to the to-do list ourselves. As we pray through our schedule asking for direction, He is faithful to give wisdom in knowing where to back off and where to press on. It's good to encourage our husbands to do the same thing.

Would it surprise you to find out that some say almost half of pastors have experienced burnout to the extent that they had to take a sabbatical from the ministry? There are times when stepping back a bit is the best way to move forward. These bodies and minds have limitations. If we continually ignore them, we can end up burned out, depressed—getting nowhere. Stepping back doesn't mean we stop loving Jesus. It doesn't even mean we stop serving Him. We never give up on those things. It just means our service may look a bit different while our minds and bodies and spirits heal. God's Word is great solace and an integral part of that healing process.

Know this. He can heal your tired heart. He'll give you the strength you need to do all He's calling you to do. "He who calls you is faithful; he will surely do it" (1 Thessalonians 5:24 ESV). There's such blessing in fulfilling that calling. Talk about deliciously invigorating. It's more energizing than the strongest mocha. With nary a carb left over! Because obviously some carbs are more complex than others.

P-Dub to P-Dub with TERI LYNNE UNDERWOOD

A few years ago my associate pastor husband and I were, as we say in the South, "give out." He was serving at a growing church, and I was "coming alongside" him as best I could while also volunteering at our local crisis pregnancy center and leading two mentor groups in our church. Like many ministry families, we were burning our candle at both ends, and when the flames finally met, it was a mess. We had given more than we had and were functioning on fumes. It wasn't pretty, and it wasn't fun.

We reached the end of ourselves and realized we had been trying to do and serve and lead out of our own strength and abilities rather than the Lord's. It was not our best season. Spiritually, we were unfocused. Physically, we were exhausted. Emotionally, we were disconnected. And mentally, we were drained.

Looking back I can see how we got there. We said yes too often. We didn't check with each other before we said the too many yeses. We allowed a perceived obligation to those outside our home to overwhelm the real obligation we had to our family.

P-DUB PARTNER-LINK: http://www.youtube.com /watch?v=GSnOd-lezbY&feature=youtu.be

You can find an easy link at rhondarhea.com at the P-Dub tab.

P-DUB POSTSCRIPTS

Passages to Plug In

The Lord is my strength and my shield; my heart trusts in Him, and I am helped. Therefore my heart rejoices, and I praise Him with my song. The Lord is the strength of His people; He is a stronghold of salvation for His anointed. Save Your people, bless Your possession, shepherd them, and carry them forever (Psalm 28:7–9).

Ponderings to Pose

Teri Lynne Underwood describes a time of being utterly overwhelmed. Ever felt that way? We need to ponder a few of the burnout signs from time to time. Here's a quick summary. Anything need attention?

• Becoming weary down to the soul, a tiredness that may even include physical aches and pains.

• Underappreciation tops a long list of disheartened feelings, and you find yourself feeling like nothing you're doing is making a difference.

• Resentment builds—even in the areas where you once found joy. There's a greater desire to isolate, and you find yourself not caring as much about people in general.

• Negativity is the order of the day. You're constantly fighting those "dark cloud" negative feelings of loneliness, cynicism, and hopelessness.

STOP, DROP, AND ROLL

If you see any hints of burnout, here's a summary of how to be ready to "stop, drop, and roll":

• STOP and examine the situation. Burnout is a sign something is wrong and needs to change. You might need to check in with your doctor. We all need to evaluate our eating and activity routines too. I know, I know. This from the Whipped Cream Queen. Sometimes, though, one of those "dark clouds" has its origins in the physical. Also, keep on fighting that urge to isolate. Ask the Lord to help you continue to plug into godly people.

• DROP some of the calendar clutter. Clear a few things off the schedule and give your spirit a chance to heal and be refreshed. Say a few nos. You probably need to pace yourself a bit better anyway. Remember, if we don't have time or energy to get everything done, we're probably doing more than the Lord has called us to do. Ask for His clear direction.

• ROLL with a fresh plan: His. There's only one who can truly meet your needs and reignite your heart. Be honest with Him about how you're feeling. Give up trying to control what you can't control. Give it all over to the ultimate Controller. Know that He can restore every broken place and that's exactly what He wants to do. Immerse yourself in His Word and in significant times of prayer. Those connections are your lifeline.

Petitions to Pray

Pray through the "burn" warning signs. Praise God for each one where you're experiencing victory. Ask for that victory for any you're dealing with now. Then go through the prayer points built into each of the stop, drop, and roll suggestions. Ask Him to keep you burning bright in all the right ways.

CHAPTER 14

Don't You Be Messin' with My Man

Let the air out of their tires? Key their cars? What are we supposed to do when someone is on the warpath against our husbands?

DON'T EVEN TRY TO PRETEND. Don't pretend you don't know that the hamburger and the french fries have to come to an end at exactly the same time. Bite of hamburger. Bite of fry. Burger. Fry. Once you invest your money in the full meal deal, it feels like bad stewardship if any one bite doesn't live up to the others. Burger, fry, burger, fry. These are the rules, people. Hey, it's not like I make this stuff up.

When you think about it, it's the only cultured way to eat a burger.

YOU CAN KETCHUP MORE FRIES WITH MONEY

Of course, "culture" and "full meal deal" don't always go together like . . . well, like burgers and fries. I hardly ever feel the need to go formal when I have that salty-grease glow all over my face. We're not exactly talking about tenderloin tartare here.

I was eating my burger, fry, burger, fry the other day, and I happened to glance over at the ketchup packet and noticed it said "fancy." Well that was just frustrating. I felt underdressed the whole rest of the meal. And I probably don't have to tell you that you want to feel well-dressed when you have to go back for that extra order of fries. Because when you're explaining to the kid taking your money that you had too much burger at the end of your fries, you don't want to look stupid.

WOULD YOU LIKE LIES WITH THAT?

When it comes to dealing well with people who are on the warpath against our husbands or telling lies about them, it can be even more challenging not to get stupid. I wish I could tell you I've never had the urge to strike back. "I have a bone to pick with you, Deacon Busybody. Looky. You've gone and gotten the paint of your car all over my key."

OK, that only happened in my head, but still.

People are going to criticize your husband. If there are two possible opinions, we'll have three coming at us at any one time. People are different. They also tend to think that they're always right. Add a fleshly sin nature to that and you have the makings for the full meal deal when it comes to disapproval, disagreement, and criticism. And as wives, we can find that awfully hard to swallow.

"He doesn't spend enough time discipling us because he's always out trying to win others." "He's way too soft on evangelism because he's spending too much time with the people who are already saved." Sometimes your poor hubby just can't win.

HUMILITY IS "KEY"

Will it comfort you to know that you and your hubs are in good, humble company? Moses caught the critical end of even those closest to him. Been there?

> *Miriam and Aaron criticized Moses because of the Cushite woman he married (for he had married a Cushite woman). They said, 'Does the Lord speak only through Moses? Does He not also speak through us?' And the Lord heard it. Moses was a very humble man, more so than any man on the face of the earth* (Numbers 12:1-3).

It's no small thing to get called out by the Lord God. It says in verse 9 that "The Lord's anger burned against them." When the Lord left, Miriam's skin was white with disease.

CHECK, PLEASE

Anytime I read that passage and I find that my favorite part is the part where Miriam and Aaron are called out and severely punished by God, I have to do an attitude check. Unjustly critical people aren't always publicly reproved for their offenses. Not always in my here and now. My favorite part of the passage really should simply be the reminder that "the Lord heard it" (v. 2). And that's enough.

God sees and hears any and every injustice committed against your husband. He knows about it and He cares. Our Father loves justice, and He loves your husband. So you can trust that in the end, without a doubt, justice will prevail. Psalm 33:5 says, "He loves righteousness and justice; the earth is full of the Lord's unfailing love."

Those who speak evil against your husband? No worries. They'll get theirs. It's not part of our job description to try to make that happen. As a matter of fact, when we do try to force the justice of God, we usually make a big, fat, bitter mess. Because we're not God. And when we try to act like we are, we really do look stupid.

WHERE'S THE BEEF?

If someone tries to speak ill of our husbands to us personally, usually all that's required of us is a referral. We can remain loyal without taking up that offense and going on the attack. We can ask that person to take the beef directly to our husband. Without reaching for our car keys and heading to the parking lot. The Lord will hold us accountable for a bad reaction the same as He will hold the attackers accountable for their offenses. Vengeance is always His. "Do not take revenge, my dear friends, but leave room for God's wrath, for it is written: 'It is mine to avenge; I will repay,' says the Lord" (Romans 12:19 NIV).

The declaration of Moses' humility sits right in the middle of Aaron and Miriam's accusation and God's judgment. For me, that's humbling. Humility should be my first response too. Moses' humility is the kind that goes a step beyond. If you go back and read the passage in Numbers 12, you'll find that Moses actually goes to God and begs for Miriam's healing. Wow, that *is* humility.

That's the kind of response that helps us guard our hearts against bitterness. Loyalty to our husband, always, but forgiveness and patience with the people we minister to—those are the order of the day. Every day.

It's our call to remember to handle criticism with class—God's kind of cultured response. And also remember, if ever you've ordered a burger and find yourself feeling a little uncultured . . . ketchup. It's the classy condiment. Anything else just won't cut the mustard.

P-Dub to P-Dub with STEPHANIE SHOTT
No! They did not say that! They obviously don't know my husband, and they certainly don't know his heart!

With my blood boiling and my claws out, I desperately wanted to defend my man. I knew it was coming, but he had only been a pastor for a week when the mudslinging started and an unfaithful few decided to behave badly.

You can mess with me, but don't mess with my kids, and don't you go messin' with my man!

I struggled to keep my head up and my mouth shut while a handful of the flock acted more like goats than sheep. It was hard to listen to the lies that hurt my hubby's heart and threatened to zap his zeal. But that's what a good pastor's wife is supposed to do, right? Unfortunately, my heart was pitching a silent fit, and all I wanted to do was straighten those ol' goats out. But the Lord reminded me that He was the One who fights our battles. Our job is to stand. And so we stood, He fought for us, the ruckus was rectified and the Lord won.

I'm still learning to keep my claws in and my mouth shut, but I know the Lord not only goes before us, but He's got our backs too. He always has. He always will. "The Lord will fight for you, and you shall hold your peace" (Exodus 14:14 NKJV).

P-DUB PARTNER-LINK: http://youtu.be/KCGGqAvo2hg
You can find an easy link at rhondarhea.com at the P-Dub tab.

P-DUB POSTSCRIPTS

Passages to Plug In

The Lord looks down from heaven and sees the whole human race. From his throne he observes all who live on the earth. He made their hearts, so he understands everything they do. The best-equipped army cannot save a king, nor is great strength enough to save a warrior. Don't count on your warhorse to give you victory—for all its strength, it cannot save you. But the Lord watches over those who fear him, those who rely on his unfailing love. He rescues them from death and keeps them alive in times of famine. We put our hope in the Lord. He is our help and our shield. In him our hearts rejoice, for we trust in his holy name. Let your unfailing love surround us, Lord, for our hope is in you alone (Psalm 33:13–22 NLT).

Ponderings to Pose

Stephanie Shott directs us to Exodus 14:14. What usually ends up happening when we sense the Lord telling us to hold our peace and we don't? Have there been times you felt you should've held your peace but didn't? What do you think it means to trust the Lord to fight for you?

Petitions to Pray

Psalm 33:13–22 in the Passages to Plug In reminds us that God is big enough to see what's happening and big enough to take care of it. Pray through the passage, praising the Lord who sees every situation you and your husband find yourselves in. Praise the God who understands. Ask Him to help you remember to rely on His strength and nothing else.

Ask Him to help you fear and honor Him and rely on His unfailing love. Cry out for rescue in every place you or your husband need it. Put your hope in Him. Praise Him that He is your help and your shield. Ask Him to cause your heart to rejoice as you trust in His holy name.

Let your unfailing love surround us, Lord, for our hope is in you alone.

CHAPTER 15

Family Time—Now Where Did I Put That?

Investing in our marriages, investing in our children—two more ways of investing in the kingdom.

MY HUSBAND SAID HIS CAR was making a weird noise. When I drove it the other day, I just turned the radio up really loud. Wow, who knew I could fix cars?

Fixing things just comes naturally for some of us I guess. I work the same kind of magic with home appliances. I try not to get all crazy when the washing machine goes into that over-the-top agitation mode, for instance—even when it sounds like the entire west side of the house is being demolished. I don't overact mostly because I'm pretty sure the machine can smell fear. And sometimes my magic is a little mixed up anyway.

PRESTO-POCUS, ABRA-KAZAM

You really don't want to aggravate the washer or dryer. The dryer is especially notorious for setting us up for some embarrassing laundry moments. One of my teacher friends said she was in a crowded hallway at school with several elementary classes all lined up. She saw one of the first-graders tugging near the shoulder of one of the sleeves of his long-sleeved T-shirt. His face was scrunched into one of those "what *is* this?" faces.

Despite all the activity around him, he kept working on whatever was troubling him until he worked it out the end of the sleeve. That's when, lo and behold, abracadabra, he pulled out a pair of his mom's panties. Then he just stood there blinking, staring in disbelief. His teacher was a little shocked when she looked over at him. She asked him what in the world he was doing standing there staring at a pair of women's underwear. He answered with no small amount of wonder and incredulity, "I have no idea."

Don't you wonder if the poor kid is now in counseling?

NOTHING UP MY SLEEVE

Anytime I happen to do a magic trick, I do hope I know it's going to happen before it does.

Between weird car noises and weirder laundry situations, between the meetings and the activities, between this need and that demand, it can start to feel like it's going to take a bit of magic to subdue the family schedule. The meaningful kind of time for family can get lost in the shuffle.

The irony is never lost on me—how we can be all about the ministry of leading people to find closeness to Jesus, and then let all the busyness and all the demands of that ministry crowd out coming close to Him as a family ourselves. We know our family is our ministry of ministries. And yet it's still so easy to let it take a backseat to the other good things we're trying to accomplish. It's like it happens almost without our knowing—as unanticipated as underwear up a sleeve.

WHAT KIND OF WEIRD MAGIC IS THIS?

Investing time in convincing our husbands that home is a harassment-free zone — there's magic there. OK, it's not really magic at all. But it is powerful. We talked about ways to invest in chapter 11. It would be nice to think we never needed reminders, but let's be real. We do. We need to commit to those refreshers. And to doing everything we can to keep our marriages strong and Jesus-focused.

As PKs our children also get to see all the best of ministry life. And all the worst. We can be their balance as we point out to them the beauty of the things of Christ and the beauty of our salvation in Him. It doesn't really take a lot of magic there either. But it does require some intention. Our response to the bests and worsts they see will influence how they deal with challenges, victories, heartaches, and joys all their lives. When we model dealing with all those things through God's Word and according to His grace, we give them a firm foundation — a secure, constant, never-changing underpinning for life and faith and all things church and ministry. Deb Mashburn speaks of the influence of grace her p-dub mom (Janet McGlaughlin in chap. 12) had on her life in the P-Dub to P-Dub in this chapter. That grace influenced Deb all the way to the missions field in Africa — and influenced her Jesus-loving siblings, as well as many others.

THERE'S FAMILY TIME AND THEN THERE'S *FAMILY TIME*

The "family time" part of family time — time together reading God's Word and praying together — is so vital to a healthy marriage and to raising kids with a balanced and positive view of ministry life. And not only the time we set aside for family worship—which is essential, of course—but the "teaching as you go" opportunities as well.

> *These words that I am giving you today are to be in your heart. Repeat them to your children. Talk about them when you sit in your house and when you walk along the road, when you lie down and when you get up. Bind the as a sign on your hand and let them be a symbol on your forehead. Write them on the doorposts of your house and on your gates* (Deuteronomy 6:6–9).

We simply can't let ourselves get too busy to make the time to let our children know we treasure the Word of God, to memorize it together, make up songs about it, read it, and talk about it together. At the breakfast table, in the minivan, in the bleachers, before bedtime—all "along the road." They need to see that time with the Lord is a priority for our family and our own personal priority as well.

WORKS LIKE MAGIC

Are there days we'll mess up? Oh yes. Days when we don't communicate grace and the blessing of Christ's church? Yes, again. Praise the God who gives better-than-any-magic grace to cover our ungraciousness. It always works. Our goal remains that our marriage will be a priority and that our children see and know and find security in the knowledge that together we choose to stand for Christ—to love Him and serve Him with everything we've got. "But as for me and my house, we will serve the Lord" (Joshua 24:15 ESV).

The best way to help our children avoid the need for heavy-duty counseling when they're older? Make family a priority and live the surrendered life before them.

But at least if they end up needing counseling anyway, there's a chance they'll have the company of panty-sleeve boy.

P-Dub to P-Dub with DEB MASHBURN

Early on in our family life, we recognized that we would have our children at home with us for just a short time. We realized spending time with them and investing in their lives had to be a priority. In addition to our two boys, we adopted two daughters and another son from Africa. The girls didn't speak English, and our new son was eight and a half and had never been to school, so he couldn't read or write. With two working parents and five active children, finding time for family wasn't always easy. Brad and I worked to get to know teachers and coaches and attended games and events as a family. We also had sit-down dinners together and made a big deal of our family time. Bedtime routine was always in place, reading, and spending time praying together.

Growing up as a pastor's daughter was great training ground for life as a missionary. My mother was amazing at being a pastor's wife. She was the mother of six, taught school, and worked tirelessly at church. She was often my dad's eyes and ears, and she visited the sick and the poor and regularly took in strangers. She was like Superwoman, and she did it all so gracefully.

A homeless man in the community often came by. She would always make him dinner and fix him a place to sleep on the couch. In appreciation for her hospitality, one week he brought her a gift. It was the hindquarter of a deer.

A roadkill deer. My mom? She graciously accepted the gift and carried it off to the garage. She never stopped modeling grace before me. Though I heard she didn't really eat the roadkill.

P-DUB PARTNER-LINK: http://youtu.be/m6dI68-Xbfk

You can find an easy link at rhondarhea.com at the P-Dub tab.

P-DUB POSTSCRIPTS

Passages to Plug In

And you shall love the Lord you God with all your [mind and] heart and with your entire being and with all your might. And these words which I am commanding you this day shall be [first] in your [own] minds and hearts; [then] you shall whet and sharpen them so as to make them penetrate, and teach and impress them diligently upon the [minds and] hearts of your children, and shall talk of them when you sit in your house and when you walk by the way, and when you lie down and when you rise up. And you shall bind them as a sign upon your hand, and they shall be as frontlets (forehead bands) between your eyes. And you shall write them upon the doorposts of your house and on your gates (Deuteronomy 6:5–9 AMP).

Ponderings to Pose

Deb Mashburn understood early on the priority of family life. When we look at Deuteronomy 6:5–9 in the Amplified Bible above, it reads like a to-do list for a balanced life, both for ourselves and for our families. Verse 7 refers to the commands of God that we are to "impress" diligently on our children. It's healthy for us to ask ourselves regularly what kind of "impression" we're making on our children. On our husbands. On our churches and those to whom we minister. And on those who don't know Jesus too. Ready for an impression inventory?

Petitions to Pray

Let's personalize the Deuteronomy 6 passage and pray it to the God of our families:

- Help me to love You with all my mind and heart, my entire being, all my might.
- Make Your commands first in my mind and heart.
- Help me to impress them on my family.
- Let my words be full of You in every moment I'm in my home.
- Everywhere my feet take me, may I reflect Your love and grace.
- When I go to bed at night, may my heart be right and my mind be on You.
- When I get up in the morning, be my first thought.
- Whatever my hands do and my eyes see—and whatever others see in me, O Lord, let it be all about You and Your amazing plan of loving redemption.
- Doorposts, gates, stem to stern, may our home be full of Your Word. May Your will be done in my life and my home.

CHAPTER 16

But Really I'm Just in This for the Money

Reassurance in the challenges of bivocational and small-salaried works and encouragement in living on a tight budget.

MAYBE I MENTIONED BEFORE THAT I always keep dried fruit in my desk drawer so I'll have a healthy snack handy when I'm working. Except the fruits are so dry that all that's left of them is these nacho cheesy Doritos.

Somehow that makes it an even sadder snack situation when I reach for my fruit and all I find in the bottom of the Doritos bag is a bunch of orange powder. I hate that. Some people would suggest that whenever that happens, I would do well to take the hint and go get an apple. Those are the people who just don't get me at all.

Then there are others who say the nacho powder is the best part. They're closer to getting me than the apple group. Still, they would no doubt think it wasteful of me if they saw me throwing away a perfectly good bag of Dorito-dust. I'm sorry, but once I find anything in my snack stash in ash form, I toss it. Definitely time for a new bag of Dor-fruit-os. Holding on to the bag when its contents are practically an aerosol just doesn't work for me. Spray-on Doritos? No, I say give the bag a decent burial and let it go. Stashes to ashes, dust to Doritos.

HOLD ON FOR DEAR LIFE

Sort of relatedly, our walk with Christ can be either wonderfully encouraged, or it can be sadly thwarted by what we choose to hang on to. And what we don't. Hang on to money or material things, success or control, popularity or fame, comfort or entertainment—or a gazillion other things that promise to satisfy but don't deliver—and there's going to be disappointment.

I know what you're thinking. Some of those disappointments are bigger than others. Some knew that the ministry life could very well be fraught with financial challenges. Some didn't see it coming. It's not fun when financial stresses are added to all the other stresses of ministry life. Don't you hate it when you're on a shoestring budget and you feel like your shoestring just broke?

That's when it's all the more urgent to look at what we're hanging on to. I certainly won't make light of the exasperation of balancing a tight budget. Not to mention high-dollar expectations from some people (i.e., people who expect you to dress like a million bucks). Then there are others who think if you have nice clothes or a nice home you're overpaid. Exasperation mounts.

MATERIALISM? CAN'T AFFORD IT

The truth is, many will always deal with those exasperations and challenges. If you're battling money aggravations, let me tell you, you're not alone. Happily, some are well-compensated. But the majority of those in ministry feel frustrated with their salary.

How we respond to those frustrations shows what we're really made of. And another truth is, no one, not one single person on this planet, has an existence that's completely exasperation-free. We can't afford to let the exasperation get the better of us. The second we do, we're launched headlong into a life completely out of focus—focusing on things instead of Christ and our calling.

Additionally, if we hang on to greed or pride, or any other sin for that matter, we inevitably find there's not only disappointment but also devastation. And as we hang on to those sins, they also begin to hang on to us. I've found that sins don't bounce off us because we're ministers' wives. It's scary-amazing how easily sin can get a hold on us, isn't it?

We need to remember that attitude counts too. "Shepherd the flock of God that is among you, exercising oversight, not under compulsion, but willingly, as God would have you; not for shameful gain, but eagerly" (1 Peter 5:2 ESV).

NOW HOLD ON THERE

Even hanging on to good things can sidetrack our lives in a fruitless direction. Jesus said, "If you try to hang on to your life, you will lose it. But if you give up your life for my sake, you will save it" (Matthew 16:25 NLT). Holding on to anything in this life is letting go of too much of Jesus. That leads to a dead-end life with no fruit. None. Not even the dried up fruit of the Doritos variety.

So much of the victorious life in Christ is about knowing when to let go and when to hold on. We're told in Deuteronomy 13:4, "Follow the Lord your God and fear Him. Keep His Laws, and listen to His voice. Work for Him, and hold on to Him" (NLV).

As we hold on to Him and passionately embrace all He calls us to be and to do, life becomes exactly what it's meant to be. It becomes sweet. It becomes dear. So you could rightly say that holding on to the Father is very surely holding on for dear life.

P-Dub to P-Dub with JAMIE HITT

When Greg and I responded to God's call to the ministry, we were comfortable with Greg hanging on to his day job. Being bivocational was a good fit. Throughout our years in ministry, we've experienced many things — some leaving us wondering just what God was thinking when He called us into ministry. But being bivocational doesn't affect the way we sing our hearts out for the Lord. And we've still had bills to pay and kids to raise.

Some people haven't understood. There have been times when someone would ask, "Are you full-time?" and after our response, we felt we didn't have the same respect. I'm sad to say, we've often walked away from those kinds of encounters feeling inferior just because of the bivocational label.

Singing for financial gain could be an easy trap to fall into as well. Either way, we have to balance singing strictly for the Lord or performing for people. To be honest, there was a time we wanted fame and money. We are human. But we had to come to a point in our ministry and in our own hearts and lives where God — and pleasing *Him* alone — became more important to us than singing or money or anything else. That was a tough time. But when we put God front and center and the music in the background, the focus of our ministry totally changed. The musical material also changed. We changed. And that was when God really began to use us for *His* glory.

P-DUB PARTNER-LINK: http://youtu.be/VnxlPgEFhnY

You can find an easy link at rhondarhea.com at the P-Dub tab.

P-DUB POSTSCRIPTS

Passages to Plug In

Turn my heart to Your decrees and not to material gain. Turn my eyes from looking at what is worthless; give me life in Your ways. Confirm what You said to Your servant, for it produces reverence for You. Turn away the disgrace I dread; indeed, Your judgments are good. How I long for Your precepts! Give me life through Your righteousness (Psalm 119:36–40).

Ponderings to Pose

Even when we think we have a handle on this area of life, the world is still constantly dangling shiny but worthless things in front of us to suck us right back into discontentment. The Passage to Plug In tells us where we have to put our eyes when that happens. Take a look at Proverbs 28:25 as well: "The greedy stir up conflict, but those who trust in the Lord will prosper" (NIV). Think for a minute about the contrast between the life focused on those shiny things and life focused on His provision. Jamie Hitt's life changed when she and her husband put the Lord "front and center." What are some ways putting the Lord front and center has changed your outlook about finances, and what do you think it means to "prosper" Proverbs 28:25 style?

Petitions to Pray

As with a lot of areas where we might find ourselves disgruntled, thanksgiving can overshadow some of those financial frustrations. Acts 14:17 (NIV) says, "Yet he has not left himself without testimony: He has shown kindness by giving you rain from heaven and crops in their seasons; he provides you with plenty of food and fills your hearts with joy."

- Pray through your own "rain" and "crops" and "food" — whatever form they take in your life. Thank the Father for all the things He provides.
- Thank Him for the joy that fills our hearts because of who He is.
- Go ahead and ask Him to bless you financially. That's really OK. We're instructed in Scripture to ask Him to meet our needs.
- Let Him know you will trust Him in deciding what those needs are—and that you will continue to thank Him, the God who bought our salvation with the blood of His own Son.

CHAPTER 17

When Christians Are Unchristian

What do we do when someone sins against us? Our husband? Our children? Confronting sin without sinning—now that's tricky.

I READ SOMEWHERE THAT THE reason shopping malls have benches is so that men can have somewhere to sit while they give up the will to live. I wonder how often guys have said the words, "I will give you 500 bucks right here on the spot if you'll just pick a pair of shoes right now. *Any pair.*"

Of course, any man who says that doesn't understand that as the words are coming out of his mouth, the savvy woman shopper is already calculating how many more pairs of shoes that will buy. The poor guy doesn't understand that he's actually buying himself at least four more shoe-shopping trips. To the mall. Most guys just don't get shoe math.

DON'T GO THERE

We all have places in life we don't particularly like to go. There are things that happen we'd simply rather not experience. That comes along with living in a world that groans under the curse of sin.

When someone sins against our husbands, against us or against our children, the challenge to hang onto our joy is even greater. And to keep from falling into sin ourselves. Many times, it's not our place to confront. Most often, if someone is sinning against my husband, for instance, I need to let that stay between the two of them and do my best not to take up that offense. I do share in the job of protecting my children, though. And allowing someone to sin against them—or against anyone—in my presence doesn't benefit anyone. When it is my place to confront, I need to do it the Jesus way.

COULD I BE BRUTALLY HONEST?

I've noticed that when people ask if they can be brutally honest, not only do they not wait for a response, but they're also usually much more about the "brutally" than the "honest." We're called to confront differently. And we're called to keep the brutality altogether out of it.

The Lord calls us to confront in a way that's not about satisfying our own sense of vengeance. Let's be "brutally honest." Sometimes we want to let people know how they've hurt us or how they've wounded someone we love. We'd love to give them what for. We want them to feel at least as badly as they've made the one they've offended feel.

Jesus calls us to confront with a whole different outcome in mind. Restoration. He said in Matthew 18:15, "If your fellow believer sins against you, go and tell him in private what he did wrong. If he listens to you, you have helped that person to be your brother or sister again" (NCV).

FAMILY FEUDS

Believers are family. And every family has its offenses and hurts. Jesus calls us to shoot for the goal of restoring every offender to be a "brother or sister again." We're told in this passage to go privately to the offending person, one to one, before we do anything else. That means before we talk to anyone else about it. If we talk to others about it before we take it to our brother or sister, we've officially become gossips.

We're also called to confront with humility. "Brethren, if any person is overtaken in misconduct or sin of any sort, you who are spiritual [who are responsive to and controlled by the Spirit] should set him right and restore and reinstate him, without any sense of superiority and with all gentleness, keeping an attentive eye on yourself, lest you should be tempted also" (Galatians 6:1 AMP). Humility, gentleness—and always remembering that we're not perfect either.

TRUTH IN LOVE

Paul teaches us in Ephesians 4:15 about dealing with people. "Instead, we will speak the truth in love, growing in every way more and more like Christ, who is the head of his body, the church" (Ephesians 4:15 NLT).

When we're told to speak the truth, that's a good reminder that we don't need to confront someone on the basis of a rumor. If we do that, we've come right back around to being more of a gossip than a woman who ministers in Christ's church. And it means we're to speak without manipulation or trying to make the offense bigger than it is.

The Greek word for "truth" in Ephesians 4:15 is about even more than our words. It implies having a life that's totally influenced and completely enveloped by truth. *Living* the truth, as it were.

We're also told to speak in love. Even when we don't feel it. How good it is to remember that at every place we don't feel the love, the Holy Spirit can fill us with it! He can give us the words of love we don't have. He is faithful to remind us that when we confront in love, our goal is not to make people suffer needlessly. It's to lead them to repentance.

Incidentally, it's kind of like that horse-and-water thing. You can lead a person to repentance, but you can't force them to do it. And that's not our job anyway. Our job is to speak the truth, to speak it humbly and with love and then trust the Lord enough to walk away and let Him work. Sometimes people respond well. Sometimes they don't. If they don't respond well, we need to remember that it doesn't mean we've failed.

NOW HANG ON JUST A MINUTE

The truth is, dealing with people is always going to be messy. We're messy people. Some may be messier than others. I love the part of Ephesians 4:15 where Paul reminds us that when we do things God's way, we're "growing in every way more and more like Christ." What joy we find there! And when we're growing more like Him, we're able to deal with the messiness of people more like He does. Our amazing Jesus loved people—even at their messiest. He loved them all the way to the Cross. And loves still.

The Savior who loves so immensely will also help you through every messy encounter with the messiest people. He's the same Savior who unconditionally loves messy you and messy me.

Hang on to your joy. Let go of animosity. Hang on to your growth in Christ. Let go of any need for revenge or retaliation. Hang on to Him.

P-Dub to P-Dub with PAULA MOWERY

My husband and I had been married about a week, maybe a week and a half. He had to return to his ministry job at the time, which was overseeing a large children's program at the church where we had married and where we were members. Because I couldn't find a use for four extra can openers and three extra toasters, I headed out to do some wedding gift exchanges. My husband's brother chauffeured me, since the mall was in a busy part of town.

Before we returned, my husband had already received calls reporting that his wife had been seen with another man—unfaithful just days after saying the vows. I was so hurt. How could these people think I would stoop so low?

But, I had to learn that being a pastor's wife is being a "public figure." Unfortunately, sometimes people will think the worst before they think anything else, so I have to consider how I appear to others who are always watching. Many Hollywood stars and sports figures say they never asked to be in the limelight or be a role model, but they are. Just as we pastors' wives are in the limelight, whether we want to be or not. I have to always consider—just as the Bible instructs—whether what I'm doing or saying would have the potential to make someone stumble. I had to let the Lord turn hurt feelings into a lesson to live by.

P-DUB PARTNER-LINK: http://www.youtube.com /watch?v=EMEdiq-I93A

You can find an easy link at rhondarhea.com at the P-Dub tab.

P-DUB POSTSCRIPTS

Passages to Plug In

Dear brothers and sisters, if another believer is overcome by some sin, you who are godly should gently and humbly help that person back onto the right path. And be careful not to fall into the same temptation yourself. Share each other's burdens, and in this way obey the law of Christ. If you think you are too important to help someone, you are only fooling yourself. You are not that important (Galatians 6:1–3 NLT).

Ponderings to Pose

Have you ever seen what happens when someone deals with an offense publicly when it should have been a private matter? Have you seen someone deal with an offense in pride, not in humility? Have you seen offenses snowball into huge battles over things that weren't even true? Have you seen people deal with an offense in all the right ways, but harshly, without love? It doesn't take a lot of pondering to know that leaving out any one element of God's formula for confrontation can make a big, fat mess. Compare that kind of mess with the love we're instructed to show "1 Corinthians 13 style." Let's read through 1 Corinthians 13 and let the Lord use it to conform our way of dealing with messy people all the more to His way.

Petitions to Pray

- Ask the Lord to give you a heart of courage to stand up and confront when you need to.

- Ask Him to give you wisdom and to give you discretion in not making public things that don't need to be public.
- Ask Him to give you humility, understanding that you've sinned too, and to help you remember that you're not too important to deal with a person who needs to better understand the truth.
- Ask Him to help you deal only in truth, not manipulation or with half-truths of any kind.
- Ask Him to give you a tender and loving heart to influence every word you communicate.

CHAPTER 18

Great Expectations

What do we do with all the expectations from others—the reasonable ones and the unreasonable ones?

YOU KNOW HOW I USUALLY know I've been too busy? I open the refrigerator door and find fur. And then I stand there for several seconds wondering what it used to be. Then I stand there another several seconds wondering if I should have it spayed or neutered.

It happened again the other day. I was standing with the fridge door open and my son told me he heard something groaning. I assured him it was only me. *They heard my groaning, yet there is no one to comfort me. For I must clean the refrigerator myself.*

That's from Lamentations 1:21. Except I added the entire last sentence.

At the point I start rewriting Lamentations, I usually figure out that I'm too busy and it's time to formulate another plan. Here's the part where I have to confess that my plan B is almost always exactly like my plan A—only with more coffee.

WAIT. YOU EXPECT ME TO *WHAT*?

The better plan B? It rests in the words of Jesus in Matthew 11:28–30. And actually it's much more appropriate as a plan A. "Come to me, all who labor and are heavy laden, and I will give you rest. Take my yoke upon you, and learn from me, for I am gentle and lowly in heart, and you will find rest for your souls. For my yoke is easy, and my burden is light" (ESV).

As p-dubs, there's an entirely different yoke we sometimes take on. The expectations yoke. When we make meeting the expectations of others our goal, we essentially yoke ourselves and our own success level to those others. We become enslaved by their idea of a pastor's wife. We're setting ourselves up for defeat and burnout anytime we do that because there's no one who can meet every expectation of every church member. And let's just get real here. Some of their expectations are just plain weird. We weren't even built to measure up to those.

It's funny, when we interviewed with the committee at the church where we now serve, I gave them every reason not to extend a call. Not because I didn't want to go. But because, as I told them several times, I believe in full disclosure. I gave them a long list of all the ways I'm not "the typical pastor's wife." If they had expectations of Super P-Dub, I wanted them to know from the get-go that though I like the idea of a cape (you can hide a lot of cellulite under one of those things), I don't even look good in tights. I wanted to squash as many potential disappointments as I could—no surprises.

THE YOKE'S ON ME

We need to remember that expectations are actually built into our makeup. Everyone has them. I have expectations of my church even, so it's not exactly fair if I ask my church to have none of me. The problem isn't in the fact that people have expectations of us. The problem comes when we yoke ourselves to them. When we take on their every expectation and try to fulfill each of them, we're setting ourselves up for feelings of failure, inadequacy, and frustration.

Getting a little more real here, I think there are probably times when a p-dub's problem is not so much with the expectations of others as it is a need to please people. When we find ourselves yoked to the approval of people, our self-worth is also yoked to what they think of us. And that's an uncomfortable and pretty dangerous yoke.

Paul called it. "We are not trying to please people but God, who tests our hearts" (1 Thessalonians 2:4 NIV). Then he solidly nailed it again in Galatians 1:10: "For am I now trying to win the favor of people, or God? Or am I striving to please people? If I were still trying to please people, I would not be a slave of Christ." On top of that, when we're spinning our wheels trying to meet the expectations of others, we're probably missing what the Lord is actually calling us to do—or at least we're too distracted by all the superfluous stuff that we're not fulfilling that calling nearly as effectively. We're limiting our own fruitfulness.

Don't settle for becoming what someone else expects you to be. If you do, you'll be settling for second best. Be who God has crafted and created you to be. Come under His yoke. He designed you with purpose. There's no greater joy than doing what you were crafted and designed to do.

BENDING UNDER THE BURDEN?

It's also true that we can be aware of those expectations without getting all bent out of shape by them. People will expect you to be a certain kind of minister's wife. You don't have to be angry about that. Sometimes the yoke is not so much the expectations of others as it is a p-dub's bitterness over people having them. Let them have their expectations. And decide even to be OK when you don't meet up to them. No need to let them become a yoke. And no need to let them become a burden of resentment either. That can be a whole new yoke in itself.

Whose expectations do we need to meet? His. It's a yoke that just fits. No bending or squirming under this one. It's interesting, when the Bible talks about the wives of church leaders, it doesn't really give us a list of things to do. In 1 Timothy 3:11 it's not so much what she does, but more about who she is. "Wives, too, must be worthy of respect, not slanderers, self-controlled, faithful in everything."

JUST COME

Anytime we find ourselves struggling under the weight of expectations, Jesus reminds us, "Come to Me."

Are you burdened? Your Savior waits for you. He waits for you to come. It's His desire to be your relief—your comfort and encouragement. And all you have to do is . . . come. Isn't it fascinating that any yoke I place on myself is utterly and entirely exhausting? And isn't it even more fascinating that the yoke of Christ is invigorating to the max in every little corner of my soul? Every day I need to remember to please only Him, to rest in Him. To give my soul a break, and to "come."

As far as the fridge is concerned, I would love a break there, too, but I don't see it happening. Looks like I'm going to have to knuckle down and clean it. Or maybe shave it.

P-Dub to P-Dub with KATHY THARP

Have you ever been asked, "How do you like being a pastor's wife?" What kind of a question is that? And, how do you answer that question? "Oh, it's divine!" "It would be great if it wasn't for the people." My personal, inward response is, *Uh, I don't know; how do you like being a plumber's wife? Or an accountant's wife?* I mean, what are they looking for? Certainly there is some kind of idea that they must have even to ask that question. Yes, expectations. Everyone has them. Even pastor's wives have expectations as to what we think about life in ministry or people in ministry.

I have learned that "The fear of man brings a snare, But he who trusts in the Lord will be exalted" (Proverbs 29:25 NASB). The one I must please with my life is the Lord. He designed me with a purpose and gifted me to fulfill that purpose in the body. So I must discover that purpose and giftedness and be confident of who I am in Christ and trust Him. I do (or don't do) what I do because I desire to honor the Lord and serve Him with my life, not because I am a pastor's wife. And, of course, part of that serving is supporting my husband and working together as a team—however the committee of three (God, my husband, me) decides. I must trust the Lord to direct my life in *all* the hats I wear. That is freeing!

P-DUB PARTNER-LINK: http://youtu.be/Zk_p-JRTLsU

You can find an easy link at rhondarhea.com at the P-Dub tab.

P-DUB POSTSCRIPTS

Passages to Plug In
Come to Me, all you who labor and are heavy-laden
and overburdened, and I will cause you to rest.

[I will ease and relieve and refresh your souls.]
*Take My yoke upon you and learn of Me, for I am
gentle (meek) and humble (lowly) in heart, and you
will find rest (relief and ease and refreshment and
recreation and blessed quiet) for your souls. For My
yoke is wholesome (useful, good—not harsh, hard,
sharp, or pressing, but comfortable, gracious, and
pleasant), and My burden is light and easy to be borne*
(Matthew 11:28–30 AMP).

Ponderings to Pose

Ever find yourself becoming a slave to someone else's expectations? It's easy to let it happen. The proverb that Kathy Tharp quotes calls it a "snare." How can a p-dub get free? What would the how-to steps look like for breaking out?

Petitions to Pray

If your soul has been in an upheaval over expectations you've failed to meet, spend some time in prayer settling that upheaval. The Amplified Bible version of Matthew 11:29 in the Passages to Plug In says that as you "come," you can find "relief"—and even more. Ask the Lord to show you expectations you've taken on that are not from Him. He will be faithful to reveal those things to you when you come to Him "expectantly." That's an expectation that is perfectly right. Ask Him to help you come under His yoke and praise Him for its perfect fit.

CHAPTER 19

My Own Worst Critic

Feelings of inadequacy. They so often come with the P-Dub Club membership card. What do we do with our own unreasonable expectations of ourselves?

HEY, MY FELLOW P-DUB, YOU don't have to be good at everything. I know this because I'm so not. And just look: that's birthed an entire ministry. Where would I be as a humor writer if I were good at more things? I would have no material, right? Of course, I did give birth to those five kids, just to make sure. So there is that.

It's great. My daughter had this for her Facebook status a few months ago: "Three facts about me: (1) I am currently enrolled in Swimming 101. (2) I am 1/64 Native American. (3) My Native American name is Drowns in River. Or, among some lesser-known tribes, White Girl Swallows Water."

Kaley is a physical education major and not used to encountering a physical activity she doesn't excel in. But I like it that she's mostly OK with not being perfect at swimming. I told her not to think of it as learning to be a good swimmer. I told her to think of it more as learning to be a not-drown-er.

COOKING UP SOME FIVE-LAYER PERFECTION

In one church where my husband and I served early in ministry, the senior pastor's wife really was somewhere near perfect. She was a spectacular cook—not just for her own family, but for the big events she hosted for the deacons and wives and all the ladies' events. We're talking cakes. With layers! She was an amazing Bible teacher. I wouldn't be surprised to find out she took gold in the 800-meter freestyle. This chick was the total package. She actually scrubbed her basement floor on her hands and knees. Her unfinished basement floor. And she did it regularly.

I don't cook worth beans. Not even beans. Organizing events is not my forte. I don't swim. I don't scrub my unfinished basement floor. I don't even clean the top of my refrigerator. If I can't see it, there's no dirt on it—that's my cleaning philosophy. Yes, of course I know my whole package is pathetic. She had the spiritual gift of everything. I'm pretty sure I have the spiritual gift of pathetic. But hey, I can use it like a boss.

I've made more mistakes and stupid moves in these past years of ministry than I would ever want to tell you. Recipe for disaster? Hey, I may not be a good cook, but I can cook up a disaster without even looking at the recipe. Mostly all I have to remember is that the main ingredient is me.

THE RECIPE FOR P-DUB CONTENTMENT

If we want to hang on to contentment in this p-dub life, we need to perceive the danger of comparing ourselves to other p-dubs. Our own self-critic is born there. Second Corinthians

10:12 informs us, "When they measure themselves by themselves and compare themselves with themselves, they are not wise" (NIV). The second we compare ourselves with others, we set ourselves up for a frustrating swim in our insecurities. Jealousy and envy will creep in. They can all too easily graduate into resentment—even full-blown bitterness. Then our fruit drains away.

When you meet a minister's wife who writes her own Vacation Bible School curriculum, choreographs every song for the children's springtime choir program, and makes salsa from veggies from her own garden, can you be happy for her? Or are you tempted to eat an entire fudge cake?

When you meet a minister's wife whose home is perpetually clean; who not only plays the piano but also composes the Christmas cantata annually; and who can teach compelling Bible studies in Hebrew, Greek, and a generous smattering of Aramaic, do you rejoice for her? Or do you eat your *weight* in fudge cake, then scream for a solid ten minutes into a sofa pillow?

When you meet a minister's wife who dresses her perfectly behaved children in the coordinating outfits she designed and made herself while simultaneously crafting the centerpieces for the mother/daughter brunch—the brunch she, of course, organizes and executes flawlessly—can you celebrate with her? Or are you more inclined to line up several fudge cakes, spell out her name several times in chocolate syrup, and then eat them, syllable by syllable, layer by layer?

It's really OK to rejoice in the strengths of another p-dub. It's even OK to let her strengths and successes inspire us. It's even more OK to know you don't have to *be* her. Trying to be someone we're not is exhausting. And really fattening.

I'M TOO THIS AND NOT ENOUGH THAT

Did you know that some studies and surveys have determined that about 85 percent of pastor's wives feel completely inadequate and underequipped for the task? That means there's a good chance that even Mrs. Perfect-P-Dub is likely feeling as inadequate as we are—even with her kids in those matching outfits! And personally I think the other 15 percent may have erroneously answered while under the influence of fudge cake. The fact is, *most* of us feel we're not enough this and we're too much that. "Lord, I'm too young." "I'm too old." "I'm too timid." "I'm too outspoken."

Jeremiah felt "too this and not enough that." The Lord had told Jeremiah that he was chosen to be a prophet to the nations. Jeremiah's response? "Alas, Sovereign Lord . . . I do not know how to speak; I am too young" (Jeremiah 1:6 NIV). The Lord answered him: "Don't say, 'I'm too young,' for you must go wherever I send you and say whatever I tell you. And don't be afraid of the people, for I will be with you and will protect you. I, the Lord, have spoken!" (vv. 7–8 NLT). Then do you know what happened? The Lord touched his mouth and said, "I have put my words in your mouth" (v. 9). It was perfectly right for Jeremiah to think he wasn't enough. But he didn't have to be enough. The Lord was his "enough."

And everywhere you feel inadequate for the role minister's wife, the same all-powerful God will be your "enough."

TRADING THE POOL OF INSECURITY
FOR A MOUNTAIN OF TRUST

Insecurity? We don't have to swim in it! "Those who trust in the Lord are like Mount Zion, which cannot be moved, but abides forever. As the mountains surround Jerusalem, so the Lord surrounds his people, from this time forth and forevermore" (Psalm 125:1–2 ESV). We can trade insecurity for trust. As we trust Him, we become as solid and secure as a mountain. It's beautiful that then *He* is our safe mountain. Not just a mountain. An entire range of impenetrable mountains, surrounding us in His protective care. In every second we're fully trusting, insecurity fades into the shadows.

So don't let insecurities fool you. Despite what you may think, we're all there at some time or another. Don't let them hold you back. Don't let them paralyze or defeat you. You are a mountain, surrounded by mountains! Find victory in that mountainous trust.

TRUST LIKE A BOSS

Incidentally, I told Kaley it was good to share her insecurities, but she didn't have to feel obligated to share her every weakness on Facebook. I think she took my advice. She's learning to see some of her strengths too. And maybe mix it up a little. Her status last week? "So got the hang of this chick-living-alone thing. Just saw a *giant spider in my sink*. So naturally I washed it down the drain, ran the disposal for a solid five, and moved on. Literally. I am moving. Just as soon as I stop crying. Like a boss."

P-Dub to P-Dub with MARY ENGLUND MURPHY

If you were to ask my parents if they expected perfection from me when I was a child, they would answer no! But that's not how I felt. If you were to ask the parishioners where I've served as a pastor's wife the same question, they, too, would answer with a resounding no! But too often, that's how I felt. Consequently, I've become my own worst critic, trying to live up to both the real and the perceived expectations of others.

I think the key word here is "felt." While my parents and our parishioners certainly had expectations for me, I felt like I was somehow required to live up to them. After years in the ministry I'm still learning that while we need to "become all things to all people so that by all possible means [we] might save some" (1 Corinthians 9:22 NIV). I also know, "Whatever [we] do, work at it with all [our] heart, as working for the Lord, not for human masters" (Colossians 3:23 NIV).

P-DUB PARTNER-LINK: http://www.youtube.com/watch?v=3 Ca8ZZebbB4&feature=youtu.be

You can find an easy link at rhondarhea.com at the P-Dub tab.

P-DUB POSTSCRIPTS

Passages to Plug In

I thank God because in Christ you have been made rich in every way, in all your speaking and in all your knowledge. Just as our witness about Christ has been guaranteed to you, so you have every gift from God while you wait for our Lord Jesus Christ to come again. Jesus will keep you strong until the end so that there will be no wrong in you on the day our Lord Jesus Christ comes again. God, who has called you into fellowship with his Son, Jesus Christ our Lord, is faithful (1 Corinthians 1:5–9 NCV).

Ponderings to Pose

Look again at the Passage to Plug In in 1 Corinthians. What are the riches spoken of here? How do your riches help you lighten up on yourself and dispel your insecurities? Mary Englund Murphy wisely embraces 1 Corinthians 9:22. How do we connect these two passages in the way we live?

Petitions to Pray

Spend some time thanking the Father for His enough-ness. Ask Him to touch your place of weakness and insecurity as He did Jeremiah's—and to use every one to show off His strength. Pray about every weakness of yours that has popped into your mind as you've read this. Thank Him that when you are weak, He is strong (2 Corinthians 12:10). Worship Him by placing your complete trust in His limitless strength.

CHAPTER 20

Who's Calling, Please?

Is it your husband's calling? Your calling? Whose calling is this anyway? Taking a look at the calling of Christ and what that means to every other calling.

I WAS A LITTLE UPSET the other day. I ordered a pizza online from my cell phone. And then I found out they wouldn't even fax it to my house. Honestly. Why isn't there an app for that?

When I'm even more honest, I'll admit that it troubles me that my smartphone is actually smarter than I am. In the past I've always been able to tell when my phone was out of date. I could tell by the fact that I'd just about figured out how to use it. My tech-savvy children don't believe me, but I'm not completely inept with all of the current technologies. Not all of the technologies. Why, just today I was playing Twitter and I'm pretty sure I won.

I-COUNSEL

Go ahead. Let the kids whine about how rough they have it. Then tell them how you had to walk to school in the snow, uphill both ways—with no Internet.

I was reading in Proverbs 19 the other day, and I had to chuckle a little when I got to verse 21. It says, "There are many devices in a man's heart; nevertheless the counsel of the Lord, that shall stand" (KJV). *Devices.* Yeah, those get our attention. We've got an e-this and an i-that. Here an *e*, there an *i*—everywhere an app for that.

E-i-e-i-phone.

DEVISING A PLAN — OR DEVICING A PLAN

Really the "devices" in Proverbs 19:21 are all about the plans we make in our own heads. The English Standard Version calls them "the plans in the mind." Have you ever had a plan in mind that you were all ready to plug in, only to find it wasn't what the Lord had planned? In a contest between our plans and His, I know I don't need to tell you that there is no contest at all. The verse in Proverbs says that it's *His* plan that will stand.

I've talked to a lot of ministers' wives who say they never felt "called" into the ministry. Maybe that's where you are too. You never really wanted or expected to sign on for p-dub duty. I know for a fact that some of you have even felt a bit blindsided by it. May I encourage you with a couple of thoughts? First with the reminder that His plan is . . . well, the standing one. His plan will stand. It's good. The ones we conjure up on our own are not nearly so sturdy.

Second, God knew you would be the wife of your minister-husband before either of you were born. He's not surprised about how it all came to be. You're a p-dub. And He knew you would be just the wife your husband needs to do the work of ministry.

Third, could I encourage you to embrace the calling? Truly embrace it. When the Lord called your husband into ministry, your calling from Him into ministry-wife life came right along with it. Because you and your husband are one, your husband's calling is yours too. There should be a mutual discernment; this is a call you can't screen.

And let me add that the Lord didn't mess up. He called you on purpose and with purpose. If you never embrace your calling, you'll live out your p-dub life wrestling with thoughts of what you're really supposed to be doing or thoughts that you're some kind of p-dub imposter. You're not. Squirming under your calling will steal away your effectiveness in fulfilling what you've been placed on this planet to do. When God calls, we need to answer. And we all need to get to the place where that answer is, "Here I am."

READY OR NOT, HERE I AM

I love Bobbye Cutshall's story of how her calling came before her husband even became a follower of Christ. It's at the end of this chapter—and it's an awesome testimony of God's gracious working. Some of us jumped into ministry with great enthusiasm. But whether enthusiastically embracing the call or struggling against it all the way, I have no doubt we all have times we feel unworthy of it. Or unprepared for it. Or a thousand other "uns."

Being sure of your calling will help you through the "uns." When Isaiah received his call from God, his response was "woe" and "un." "Woe is me for I am ruined because I am a man of unclean lips and live among a people of unclean lips, and because my eyes have seen the King, the Lord of Hosts" (Isaiah 6:5). The Lord God is the one who prepared Isaiah to fulfill his calling. He brought him all the way from "un" to the sure place of "Here I am. Send me" (v. 8).

NAME THEM UN BY UN

Isaiah was overwhelmed by the blazing holiness of God. That made his own unholiness so painfully, desperately obvious. But the Lord of Hosts took care of Isaiah's need for cleansing. He readied Isaiah for His call. Is there any "un" on your list He can't take care of?

We serve the same Lord of Hosts. He will ready us for our call as surely as He did Isaiah. We don't even need an app for that.

Though for the record, on the pizza side of the conversation, I'm still thinking my smart phone isn't all that smart if there's no pepperoni app.

P-Dub to P-Dub with BOBBYE CUTSHALL

I accepted Christ when I was 24, and my husband accepted Christ four years later. From the beginning I felt the Lord wanted me in some kind of full-time Christian ministry. "But, Lord, I have a husband who doesn't know You." Then later, "Lord, I have a husband who doesn't feel the same call." Then came the day, after five years as a Christian, he told me that he felt the Lord was calling him to some kind of ministry. My heart rejoiced! He still had four years of obligation to the Marine Corps and planned to go to seminary when he finished his time. When the time came, he felt we couldn't go to seminary, since we still had three children at home with one going into college.

I'll never forget the night my husband went forward in church and said, "I can't fight it anymore. The Lord has called me into the ministry. Practical or not, I can do nothing else."

We have been in the ministry now for 24 years. Whose call was it? I believe it was God's call primarily to my husband. For many years I thought it was my call first and that it just took longer to bring my husband around. But as I think back over the years and how the Lord has worked in our lives, I realize that it was me that took the long time. Time to grow into the helpmeet I needed to be for him. I had a lot of spiritual arrogance that needed to die in me before I was suitable. I do not say this to discount my calling. My calling was and is to support him in his ministry, to complete him.

P-DUB PARTNER-LINK: http://www.youtube.com /watch?v=0IftzYFxuUk&feature=em-upload_owner

You can find an easy link at rhondarhea.com at the P-Dub tab.

P-DUB POSTSCRIPTS

Passages to Plug In

Then I said:

> *Woe is me for I am ruined*
> *because I am a man of unclean lips*
> *and live among a people of unclean lips,*
> *and because my eyes have seen the King,*
> *the Lord of Hosts.*

Then one of the seraphim flew to me, and in his hand was a glowing coal that he had taken from the altar with tongs. He touched my mouth with it and said:

> *Now that this has touched your lips,*
> *your wickedness is removed*
> *and your sin is atoned for.*

Then I heard the voice of the Lord saying:

> *Who should I send?*
> *Who will go for Us?*

I said:

> *Here I am. Send me* (Isaiah 6:5–8).

Ponderings to Pose

We can hardly think about the plans of God without bringing in Jeremiah 29:11, "'For I know the plans I have for you'—this is the Lord's declaration—'plans for your welfare, not for disaster, to give you a future and a hope.'" Thinking about your calling and about the good and sturdy plan of God, how does Jeremiah 29:11 speak to whatever situation you find yourself in right now?

Petitions to Pray

Spend time thanking the Lord for your amazing calling and the honor that it is—even when it's challenging, "Here I am. Send me." We reinforce our commitment to His calling every time we pray it. Pray it today. As you're praying, ask the Lord to deal with any and every "un" by His glorious power.

CHAPTER 21

A Server with Fervor

Finding our own place of ministry where we can serve with fervor and passion—even if we can't play the piano.

WE PLAYED MONOPOLY A LOT when I was a kid. Of course, in the earliest years, playing Monopoly usually meant pretending to sew with that itsy-bitsy thimble or using the little iron to get the pretend wrinkles out of Barbie's clothes. Or sometimes it meant putting all the money in my dad's tackle box so we could play store.

By the time we were ready to play the actual game, most of the money and at least half the tokens were missing. But then we just combined what was left of the game with a few parts from Clue and Mouse Trap, and we were good to go. OK, so we did have to change a few rules. I'm pretty sure I remember a time when my brother won because he drew a cheese card and Colonel Mustard took a ride on the Reading Railroad. Though now that I think about it, my brother always seemed to win anytime he was the banker. What are the odds?

I think my favorite game of Monopoly was the one we played using Cheetos for replacement parts. The game was over whenever we finished eating it. The board was pretty orange, I won't lie, but it was about the most delicious game we ever played. I wonder if that's why I still have a bit of a thing for Cheetos. Of course, now I've matured. Instead of calling them Cheetos, I like to call them croutons. That way whatever I put them on is automatically a salad. It's no wonder, though, that I'm still a tad confused on the rules of Monopoly. Rules of salad, too, but I was confused about the rules of Monopoly first.

THIS IS NOT CHEETO-OPOLY

I think the name of the game is a little confusing even before you add the Cheetos. I know *mono* has its origins in the Greek language and means "alone" or "one." The Greek *poly* means "many," right? So which is it? One or many? I'm not sure if I need training in the rules of Monopoly or the rules of etymology.

OK, just a little jokette. I realize I'm butchering that a bit, and there are other words and origins at play here. But I don't have to stretch it too far for it to serve as a little reminder that it's good to train ourselves in how we look at our service.

"Train" ourselves. You realize that there's simply no way I can resist the urge to add a railroad pun somewhere in a Monopoly chapter, right? I'll try to at least make it a Short Line (*clearing throat*). And I figure I'll be OK as long as I don't get too far "off track." But training ourselves can be a little like riding the Reading. Or really, reading the writing. Like the words Jesus Himself said to shoo off Satan's temptation:

"You shall worship the Lord your God, and him only shall you serve" (Luke 4:8 ESV).

THE NAME OF THE GAME

We're to serve Him only, the One and the only, according to that verse. Mono-mono. One serving The One. And when we serve the One, He gives us the exact gifts we need to serve the many—and serve in just the way He planned for us. "For we are His creation, created in Christ Jesus for good works, which God prepared ahead of time so that we should walk in them" (Ephesians 2:10).

It ends up something more like Mono-mono-poly. Except it's no game. It's life. And life at its best.

ALL THE CARDS ON THE TABLE

You're gifted by God. Don't you love that? "As each has received a gift, use it to serve one another, as good stewards of God's varied grace" (1 Peter 4:10 ESV). Anytime we're not using that gift—or we're burying it away while we serve in areas where we aren't gifted, we're not being good stewards of the grace of God. He gave you that gift by His grace—a special present just for you.

What is it that the Lord has given you a passion for? What gets your juices going in ministry? What revs the engine of your little car, so to speak? It's your Heavenly Father who put those gifts and passions in you. And you will find the most incredible fulfillment in serving in those places you were designed to serve.

Do everything you can to work in those places. When we're being realistic, we all know that there will be times when we're required to serve outside our area of giftedness. That's called "duty," and everyone experiences those little stretches. But let me encourage you to let those little stretches be temporary seasons, not places you park for a long time. It may be "free parking," but it comes at a cost. Serving outside your giftedness is one of the chief causes of burnout. Conversely, it's also true that serving within your area of giftedness and using the creativity the Lord placed in you when He knit you together is absolutely energizing, even when it wears you out! It births even more creativity. It's where burnout dies and excitement in ministry burgeons.

TOGETHER IN THE SERVICE

Your gift is for the whole body. "A spiritual gift is given to each of us as a means of helping the entire church" (1 Corinthians 12:7 NLT). What a blessing it is when we serve together.

Paul gives instructions that refer to the many of us striving side by side with one mind: "Only let your manner of life be worthy of the gospel of Christ, so that whether I come and see you or am absent, I may hear of you that you are standing firm in one spirit, with one mind striving side by side for the faith of the gospel" (Philippians 1:27 ESV). Side by side — more than one — but one mind. And with one voice, according to Romans 15:6: "That you may glorify the God and Father of our Lord Jesus Christ with a united mind and voice." The many together, yet one voice. Mono, yet in stereo!

In every place where *mono* begins to feel more "alone," we can be thankful and receive great encouragement as we remember that we don't have to go it mono. God's plan is for us to work together, combining our game pieces, as it were, and we're good to go. As a matter of fact, we're good to go all the way to the uttermost parts of the world with His gospel.

As we roll up our sleeves alongside each other as servants of Christ, we see kingdom fruit. Many working for The One. *Polymono*, maybe?

Serving with passion to advance the kingdom. That's where we really win. We just do. Even if we're never the banker.

P-Dub to P-Dub with KATIE ORR

I don't work in the nursery.

Yep, you heard me correctly. No holding babies or wiping bottoms for me! (I do enough of that at home.) The nursery is not my first place of service because it's not what I'm gifted at doing. OK, so I'm not saying that certain people are gifted at wiping bottoms, but I do believe that there are many wonderfully *gifted* women who love to work with children.

I am not one of them.

Our creator has handcrafted you and me to be *unique* vessels to do His work, and to bring Him glory (Ephesians 2:10). It is important for you and me to serve in our strengths; this is especially true in the busy seasons of life.

I know that God has crafted me to lead, teach, and equip. When I serve in these gifts I come away energized. When I serve out of guilt or duty it quickly becomes draining. The cool thing is, as we lead by example through serving according to our gifting, it also frees women around us to be who God has created *them* to be.

So, go ahead and wipe those bottoms and cradle those babies, sing in the choir, help with the budget, and lead a dozen Bible studies. But not before you've taken a good look at who God has created *you* to be.

P-DUB PARTNER-LINK: http://youtu.be/dL6PLGtWcKs?t=2s

You can find an easy link at rhondarhea.com at the P-Dub tab.

P-DUB POSTSCRIPTS

Passages to Plug In

As each has received a gift, use it to serve one another, as good stewards of God's varied grace: whoever speaks, as one who speaks oracles of God; whoever serves, as one who serves by the strength that God supplies—in order that in everything God may be glorified through Jesus Christ. To him belong glory and dominion forever and ever. Amen. (1 Peter 4:10–11 ESV).

Ponderings to Pose

Katie Orr brought out a point I hadn't thought of. She mentions that when we serve where we're gifted, we're leading by example and we could actually be freeing other women to serve the way they were designed to serve. I love that! Think about your own example in serving. Do you feel free to be yourself? Do you think your example to others is encouraging freedom in them too?

Petitions to Pray

Take a gift-entory. Inventory those gifts and ask yourself where God has given you a deep passion to serve. Thank Him for the gifts and for every desire He's put in your heart to serve Him. But we certainly don't want to stop at merely asking ourselves where we should serve. We want to ask the Father.

- Where do you want me to serve?
- How can I best use the gifts you've given me to bring glory to Your name and to bless Your kingdom?
- Lord, will you please strengthen me, empower me and give me the wisdom and grace to serve You only, and to serve You by serving the people You're calling me to serve?

CHAPTER 22

Take Cover!

"Honey, how 'bout you reconsider that job on the bomb squad. Because being a pastor is just too dangerous." Explosive upheaval in our churches? It happens.

I WAS A YOUNG, SINGLE chick and had just moved to a new area a couple of hours from what had always been home. I was still trying to find my way around, so I started with the most logical place. The mall. A girl always feels at home there, right?

First things first, I found the ladies room. Then it was off for the mall adventure. I was zipping down the main drag at a pretty good clip, checking out shops in both directions. I'm a shopping supermultitasker that way. Actually, I'm a megashopping supermultitasker because I had just let the ladies' room hand soap suck all the moisture out of my hands and decided I could also dig the lotion out of my purse and lotion-up without even slowing my pace.

It was going well until I was thump-thump-thumping that little purse-sized lotion bottle on my hands—and nothing was happening. It was brand new. I knew that stuff had to be in there. Another thump, thump, thump. Still nothing. I kept up the mall-scoping pace anyway as I looked down at the top of the lotion. Yep. Little cardboard circle stuck over the opening. What possible function could that thing have?

It was pretty secure, too. I gave the bottle a little squeeze to loosen it and it didn't even budge. Another little squeeze. No give. A couple more of those, and I felt like the thing was laughing at me. So I gave it a real squeeze. I kind of wanted to hurt it.

You can probably guess where this is going. If only I had. I wrenched that thing so hard I turned it into a little lotion bazooka. There was a "puh" sound just as the little cardboard circle hit me in the forehead. It almost stuck. Totally not the worst of it. Lotion globs shot straight for the right side of my face. It was all in my hair and just about covered one eye. Pace sorely interrupted. I stopped and just stood there for a few seconds—maybe trying to let the shock wear off. Maybe trying to figure out what to do next. Maybe trying to decide what to do with the humiliation.

It got worse before it got better. That lotion didn't hang on these eyelashes for more than a second or two before I could feel the mascara giving way to the grease. So yeah, why don't we just add a black eye to the whole picture? Mercy. I pulled out my purse mirror to assess the damage. If a black-eyed zombie and a slime lagoon monster had a baby, it would be me.

I thought I might die. It would've been so much better if I hadn't been alone. Everyone needs a friend at a time like that to point, tease and fall over in uproarious mocking laughter. I did laugh. But when zombie-slime-baby laughs, it's just creepy. Mortification complete.

It only hurts if you don't laugh.

SOFTLY AND TENDERLY JESUS IS CALLING

I figure at least I left the mall with softer skin than when I went in. So there was that.

When it comes to a surprising explosion in the church, we need to stay soft and pliable to all things Jesus then too. I know. It's not always easy. Before we start plotting a strategy and before we talk to anyone else, we need to hit our knees. An upheaval should be our call to prayer. We need to talk to the Father first. I don't think we can be reminded enough what great power we find on our knees.

It's still surprising when sinners are sinful. I don't know why, but it is. Those explosive sinful events can be the most devastating. Our pace is certainly and sorely interrupted. But if we go to the Lord first, we'll find the strength to endure. Not only endure, but experience victory.

Psalm 124 is a song of ascents of David, a song they sang as he was going in to Jerusalem, victorious. David knew that if the Lord had not been for him in battle, his people would've lost and would've been completely destroyed. He knew just exactly where his victory and where his defense had come from. The Lord who made heaven and earth.

While we're living on a fallen planet where sin still has room to reign, we're going to encounter people who are bent on our destruction. When someone comes against you, who can you depend on? Do you truly realize who it is who's on your side? Your God is your defender. Your provider. Your guide. So much more. It doesn't matter how big and bad your enemy seems to be. You have the upper hand. It's not your own hand. It's His. And it can't get more "upper" than that.

STAYING SOFTHEARTED

In the notes on Psalm 124 in *Matthew Henry's Concise Commentary* we read, "God suffers the enemies of his people sometimes to prevail very far against them, that his power may be seen the more in their deliverance. Happy the people whose God is Jehovah, a God all-sufficient."

We won't always know the whys of turmoil in the church. But that's OK as long as we know He knows. And it helps to know, too, that the upheaval is typically just a season. While we're remembering, we also need to remember to stay soft. It's not always simple to keep a tough skin but a lotion-soft heart. But it's exactly what we need.

If days come when you feel that being a softhearted pastor's wife is more than you can do, step back for a minute and just love Jesus. It always starts there. Love Him and rest in Him for a bit. Then just love your husband. Sometimes in that perspective the Lord will give us the tenderness we need and keep us from becoming hardhearted.

In case you're wondering what happened to me and my mortifying lotion-face incident, even though I thought I might die, it didn't really kill me. I did, however, move again within the next year.

P-Dub to P-Dub with DIANE NIX

I had known with great clarity that God was leading us to our next place of ministry, but through my prayer time God had spoken that though this was going to be *the* place for *this* time, it was going to be anything but easy. And frankly, I knew it was in fact going to be very hard.

What an understatement! We flew high from one very successful ministry into the new church. Within the next year, tough leadership decisions, slander—lies and all kinds of maligning—and anonymous letters became daily events. There were times we questioned our giftedness and our calling.

Before, we had viewed other ministry couples struggling in their churches and thought, "If they had just led better," or "If only they would have loved more or prayed more," or "If only he would have been a stronger leader." Those thoughts changed. And I found out for myself that it's very lonely when everything explodes.

One day, my ice-cream-lovin' husband, scoop in hand, turned to me and said, "You know if I get fired from this church, I can't do anything else well except dip ice cream. You think Baskin-Robbins will hire me?"

We survived. We are forever changed for our good and God's glory.

P-DUB PARTNER-LINK: https://vimeo .com/68553371?email_id=Y2xpcF90cmFuc2NvZGVkfGI5 NmZmMWQ5ZTc1MjA3Zjg3OGEwN2FmMTcxNTg4NWE 4ODQ0fDE4MzQ0NzYxfDEzNzE0OTUwODA%3D&utm_ campaign=7701&utm_medium=clip-transcode_complete-finished-20120100&utm_source=email

You can find an easy link at rhondarhea.com at the P-Dub tab.

P-DUB POSTSCRIPTS

Passages to Plug In

If it had not been the Lord Who was on our side—now may Israel say—If it had not been the Lord Who was on our side when men rose up against us, Then they would have quickly swallowed us up alive when

their wrath was kindled against us; Then the waters would have overwhelmed us and swept us away, the torrent would have gone over us; Then the proud waters would have gone over us. Blessed be the Lord, Who has not given us as prey to their teeth! We are like a bird escaped from the snare of the fowlers; the snare is broken, and we have escaped! Our help is in the name of the Lord, Who made heaven and earth (Psalm 124:1–8 AMP).

Ponderings to Pose

Three important points to ponder from this chapter anytime we face upheaval:

• Pray first—focus on Christ, not the troubling happenings.
• Remember, it's but a season.
• Stay soft.

Find a verse or two for each point. Consider committing the verses to memory. They will help you be ready for every kind of surprise.

Petitions to Pray

Lord, help us to remember that You are our defender. You will fight the battles. And You will have the upper hand. Thank You for the strength You give for every explosive situation. O Lord, our help is ever and always in Your mighty name!

CHAPTER 23

It's Been Rumored...

We can become the church gossip-squashers.
Earning the title of "Sass-Squash" is an honor.

I WAS BORN IN TEXAS. We're mostly big sneezers there. It's widely accepted that Texans do everything bigger. No wimpy little "achoo." No, that's simply not Texan enough. It wouldn't surprise me to find out that in the enormous hair seasons, Texas keeps a law on the books that says your sneeze has to be at least as big as your hair.

My sneeze comes out in sort of a "Yah-hoo!" Heavy on the "yah" and extra, extra heavy on the "hoo." It could hardly get more Texan than that—unless maybe I roped and branded something in the middle of it.

My Texas sneeze has a heaping helping of reverberation in it too. It can give ringing ears to everyone within an eighth of a mile radius for a good ten minutes. My husband says my sneeze registers 8.7 on the Richter scale. He's exaggerating, of course. It's probably barely a 4. Just a mild sneeze-quake, if you will.

But to top it all off, my husband also tells me I always sneeze in nines. I think it's interesting that he accounts for all of them. But then maybe it's a little like counting down a missile launch. Except that it's more like a missile launch . . . times nine. He's asked that I start yelling, "Incoming!" before the first sneeze launches.

I have to admit it, reverberation is not always a good thing.

REVERBERATING RUMORS

Worse than any sneeze-quake, gossip can flat-out crumble a ministry. It jostles effectiveness to its core. There's no doubt we're instructed to get rid of it. In the qualifications for spiritual leaders section of 1 Timothy, Paul writes, "Wives, too, must be worthy of respect, not slanderers, self-controlled, faithful in everything" (1 Timothy 3:11).

Sometimes gossip can be lies. Sometimes it's spreading something around that's absolutely true but not meant to be shared. We generally know a lot of things that aren't common knowledge about people in our church or our area of ministry—things that aren't supposed to be common knowledge.

Complaining about church aggravations and church people? There's no good place for that. Do we do it anyway? Yeah. Sometimes we do. Sometimes without even realizing it.

I wish I could tell you I've never been guilty of it. But there've been far too many times, even as the Holy Spirit was tapping on my shoulder and letting me know I was heading into gossip territory, I still haven't shut up. I also know that every time I've kept talking, I've said more about my own shortcomings than whatever I said about the topic of conversation. Oh, that my tongue had more teeth-marks in it!

SASS-SQUASHER

I still have a responsibility to squash the nonsense. We all have a responsibility to squash gossip, rumors, back-biting, and all such sass. All we have to do is *don't*. We don't have to perpetuate a rumor. We don't have to allow people to share the latest juicy tidbit with us. We don't have to spill every bit of information we know. Before we speak or before we even listen, we can stop and ask ourselves if it's gossip. And if it is, we can simply don't.

When we listen to or share a rumor—even if it's something true—just to satisfy our own curiosity or to show off the fact that we're in the know, we really do whittle away at our own reputation. People need to be able to trust that we are women of character and that we're honorable and dependable—that we're trustworthy enough to keep a confidence. Proverbs 11:13 says it plainly: "A gossip goes around revealing a secret, but a trustworthy person keeps a confidence."Maturity means not feeling we have to know everything, and not feeling we have to show off everything we do know.

There are times when doing what we need to do to squash rumors means choosing carefully who we spend significant time with. Is there someone who is sort of like your spiritual ragweed, inciting you to reverberate gossip? Proverbs 20:19 says, "The one who reveals secrets is a constant gossip; avoid someone with a big mouth." If you have a tongue problem every time you're with that certain person, you may need to cancel those coffee dates. Avoid the allergens. Or you can also choose to hang out with her only in a group. There's accountability in numbers.

CAN WE TALK?

I don't know how to tell you this, but I'm a talker. Yeah, I don't know how to tell you, yet I'll still use a whole lot of words to do it. So what about people like me who find it such a challenge to shut up? My petition for His strength has to be an everyday, ongoing thing. Tongue on the altar, as it were.

"Seek the Lord and his strength; seek his presence continually!" (Psalm 105:4 ESV). The "continually" there supports being consistent in the process of tapping into His strength to make it happen, not my own. Continually—it's not just a one-time seeking. When we're caught up in the presence of Christ, gossip is thoroughly vaporized.

And that's nothing to sneeze at, for sure.

Speaking of sneezes, you're going to think I'm making this part up, but I started sneezing while I was writing this. Totally true (as in *not* a rumor). Mid–first-paragraph, even. I haven't seen the cat for over an hour.

P-Dub to P-Dub with NICOLE HUFTY

"Did you hear what Katherine did on Friday night? I think we need to pray for her." Questions such as these perk ears and lead to juicy and sometimes exaggerated information. I think we've all been in a similar situation: a group of women praying during Bible study and the prayer requests sound more like "spiritual tattle-telling" rather than sharing a prayer need.

Gossip should always end with you. If it comes to you, you have an opportunity to stop it. It may mean asking that person to address the problem with the one they are gossiping about. It is hard having those tough conversations, but they are necessary. It is much easier to criticize than to edify, but this habit becomes destructive to the body of Christ and to our personal character.

My husband is such a good example of handling rumors well. If he hears something negative circulating, he immediately goes to the source of the complaint. It usually catches the source off guard, but opens the lines of communication to constructive repair rather than destructive harboring.

P-DUB PARTNER-LINK: http://www.youtube.com/watch?v=Y tU0XxTa49E&feature=youtu.be

You can find an easy link at rhondarhea.com at the P-Dub tab.

P-DUB POSTSCRIPTS

Passages to Plug In

A word out of your mouth may seem of no account, but it can accomplish nearly anything—or destroy it! It only takes a spark, remember, to set off a forest fire. A careless or wrongly placed word out of your mouth can do that. By our speech we can ruin the world, turn harmony to chaos, throw mud on a reputation, send the whole world up in smoke and go up in smoke with it, smoke right from the pit of hell (James 3:5–6 *The Message*).

Ponderings to Pose

Nicole Hufty shares about handling rumors well and compares "constructive repair" to "destructive harboring." Our words can "accomplish nearly anything" or they can "destroy it" according to *The Message* paraphrase of James 3 in the Passages to Plug In. Are you spending more of your life in the "constructive repair/accomplish nearly anything" side of the comparisons? Are you a gossip-stopper? How does a person become one?

Petitions to Pray

Spend time giving your words to the Lord. If you've been struggling with using your words carelessly or hurtfully, ask Him to forgive you and to set you on a better word path. Ask Him to help you trade the earth-shattering destruction for victorious accomplishment. He will be your strength. Ask Him to strengthen you to use your words to bring about His purposes and to bring Him glory.

CHAPTER 24

To Work the Impossible Work: Super P-Dubbery

It's not like we're Wonder Women. Or are we? Where can we pick up our own super powers—and how can we use them for good and not evil?

SOMEBODY ASKED ME WHAT SUPER power I would want if I could have any of them. I thought about it, and then I decided on Batman's. Because as far as I can tell, Batman's superpower is this: having a fat boatload of money. That one just seemed the most reasonable.

After thinking about it a little more, I decided it was entirely conceivable that I've already been bitten by a radioactive spider. It would have to have been a spider that gives you the spider superpower of being a regular human. So now that's my superpower. You know. Being a regular human. But again, this worked out OK for Batman.

Superhuman p-dub powers? Never a question. I so obviously don't have those either. I can't leap tall fellowship hall tables—not in any number of bounds. Not even if it's to get to the dessert table.

164

I'm not going to get all bent out of shape about not being a super hero. For one thing, getting bent out of shape would make me Mr. Fantastic or Elastic Man or somebody stretchy like that. But mostly because all of that is silly pretend power. I know where the real stuff comes from. We have power available to accomplish everything worthy of accomplishing—all through the power of the Spirit of God. Through His power and according to His plan, every believer has the amazing opportunity to work for the kingdom of God. We've looked at what Paul tells us in Ephesians 2:10: "For we are his workmanship, created in Christ Jesus for good works, which God prepared beforehand, that we should walk in them" (ESV). But I so love thinking about the way every task has been long ago hand chosen for each of us individually by a loving Father.

If He hand picks each mission, why would we even for a second wonder where the power would come from to carry out each of those missions? In that same chapter in Ephesians, we're told, "In him you also are being built together into a dwelling place for God by the Spirit" (v. 22 ESV). We never lack the power to carry out whatever job He's given us to do. That power—His power—dwells in us. First Corinthians 12:6 says, "There are varieties of activities, but it is the same God who empowers them all in everyone" (ESV).

NOTHING PERSONAL

We're not talking about a person's "abilities" here. It's not our strength. Not our intelligence. Not our possessions or our money—even if we have a fat boatload of it. This power is infinitely bigger. We're empowered by the Holy Spirit of our all-powerful God. Superpowers of the highest order.

If you ever find yourself feeling inadequate for a task you believe God has called you to, let me encourage you to remember that you don't need to hesitate for a second. He will accomplish through you by His indwelling power every job He's calling you to do. No need to shy away from any task—even those that seem overwhelming in your own non-super-heroic powers.

The power to be everything you need to be as a pastor's wife, the power to love your husband, your church—even the power to share His gospel—is a super power that comes directly from the Holy Spirit. Paul gives us the order of happenings in Acts 1:8 when he says "you will receive power when the Holy Spirit comes on you; and you will be my witnesses" (NIV). I love that. No ifs there. Not a hesitation anywhere. "You will receive power."

His Spirit changes us. It's better than any super hero transformation. No radioactive spider bite needed. Don't even bother with the gamma radiation. Through the omni-power of His Spirit, we can become a powerful force for the kingdom. "The Spirit of the Lord will control you, you will prophesy with them, and you will be transformed into a different person. When these signs have happened to you, do whatever your circumstances require because God is with you" (1 Samuel 10:6–7).

So go ahead. Do "whatever your circumstances require." Whatever is required of you as a p-dub, as a mom, as a friend, as a daughter—whatever. Whatever is required of you as a child of God. Because He is with you. There is super power there of the highest order. The power to change the world is right there. And it stretches from here to eternity.

Without the slightest assistance from Mr. Fantastic.

P-Dub to P-Dub with DIANE CAMPBELL

I have a confession to make and I make it somewhat sheepishly. Wonder Woman *does* exist . . . and I am she. I'm not very proud of the fact, but it is true. Just yesterday, for instance, I walked right into the living room and I wondered, "What did I come in here for?" I used to blame it on my age, but I think I've actually always pretty much been this way.

And so, when it comes to getting all the normal things done that need getting done every day, I require some industrial-strength help. Second Corinthians 12:9 says, "My grace is sufficient for thee, for my strength is made perfect in weakness" (KJV). I figure I am the perfect candidate for that!

Each morning, by sheer necessity, I ask God to direct my steps for the day. I ask Him to give me the strength to do whatever needs to be done, to give me eyes to see things His way, and I ask that all I do would be pleasing to Him. There are literally hundreds of choices we have to make each day, and I don't want to get off track.

Help me, Lord, as we go through this day together.

P-DUB PARTNER-LINK: http://www.youtube.com/watch?v=r Le8bVR1gFg&feature=youtu.be

You can find an easy link at rhondarhea.com at the P-Dub tab.

P-DUB POSTSCRIPTS

Passages to Plug In

When I came to you, brothers, announcing the testimony of God to you, I did not come with brilliance of speech or wisdom. For I didn't think it was a good idea to know anything among you except Jesus Christ and Him crucified. I came to you in weakness, in

*fear, and in much trembling. My speech and my proc-
lamation were not with persuasive words of wisdom
but with a powerful demonstration by the Spirit, so
that your faith might not be based on men's wisdom
but on God's power* (1 Corinthians 2:1–5).

Ponderings to Pose

As you consider the passage in 1 Corinthians 2:1–5, think
about Paul's reliance. Take a second look at everything Paul
was relying on for effective, successful, joyful, mega-powered
ministry. And on what did he not rely? Is there anything God
is calling you to in ministry that you're hesitating to do? Are
there areas in which you're feeling a little powerless? What
will you do to get powered up? Would you consider praying
through the four points Diane Campbell prays as part of her
every-morning prayer routine?

Petitions to Pray

Spend a moment praising and thanking God that success in
ministry never depends on your own abilities or your own
power. What a relief!

- Help me embrace the truth that there's nothing You've
  called me to do that You will not empower me to do.
- Give me the ability to trust in Your power to do it all.
- In every little place where I feel overwhelmed and
  powerless, I ask that You will show Your power. Exchange
  those feelings of weakness for the assurance of Your
  presence and Your amazing empowering.
- Accomplish in me all that You want to accomplish—all by
  Your power.

CHAPTER 25

P-Dubs and the Cubs

Encouraging our PK's. How can we mama bears bless our children? Shield them? Build them? See them grow into followers of Christ who love Him and His church?

IF WE ACTUALLY FOLLOW THE "lather, rinse, repeat" instructions on the shampoo bottle, won't we end up stuck in a shower-time-loop for the rest of our lives? Then again, if we read the directions on a lot of these products, we might just end up *confused* for the rest of our lives. Like the can of spray paint with the label that reads, "Do not spray in your face." Wow. Barely dodged that bullet.

Then there's the blow dryer with the directions, "Do not use while sleeping." Again, whew—close one. And since we all seem to have such a difficult time figuring out how to grasp the complexities of the blow dryer, everyone will be relieved to know that there's a blowtorch out there that actually says right on the label, "Not used for drying hair."

I'm not sure why we're especially confusable when it comes to getting good hair, but there's also hair dye on a store shelf that gives us the caution, "Do not use as ice cream topping." And I thought *I* was a bad cook. I guess I must at least be better in the kitchen than some people because, believe it or not, there was actually a toaster that had to be labeled, "Do not use underwater." Ah, man. There goes all my pool-toast.

FOLLOW THE DIRECTIONS

Even though my underwater toast fun is pretty much ruined, I'm OK with sticking to my convictions to remain a conscientious follower of directions. Lathering and relathering, it's probably just a safer way to live. But so much more than any earthly directions, I want to do everything I can to ever-stick to my convictions to remain a conscientious follower of Christ. Because — it's as scary as it is true — people follow me.

As my five children have grown, it's been my heart-of-heart's desire that my example of following be one worth following. It's also been my fervent prayer that they would experience a deep love for the Lord, and that they would never resent His church. I've prayed that they would follow Jesus with everything they've got — no reservations. Tall order when you look at the PK statistics, I know.

The "following" message has been brought to you by Jesus. Jesus initiates our following. In Matthew 4 we read about Him calling the first disciples to follow.

> *While walking by the Sea of Galilee, he saw two brothers, Simon (who is called Peter) and Andrew his brother, casting a net into the sea, for they were fishermen. And he said to them, "Follow me, and I will make you fishers of men." Immediately they left their nets and followed him. And going on from there he*

saw two other brothers, James the son of Zebedee and John his brother, in the boat with Zebedee their father, mending their nets, and he called them. Immediately they left the boat and their father and followed him (Matthew 4:18–22 ESV).

Simple directions? Not really. To follow these instructions, they had first to let go of what they held on to for security. They had to let go of most everything they knew. Even people they loved. Yet each of the four "immediately" left nets, boat, father—way of life—and followed.

It's still His instruction to us today—for us and for our children. It's not always easy for us, and it's not always easy for them either. But the instructions stand. Follow. Leave the things that others tell you will bring you security. Leave the shiny distractions that attempt to thoroughly capture your fancy. Leave even some people you might be tempted to devote your time and energy and heart to. Leave the directions that outsiders give to try to convince you of their way to succeed in life. Drop those nets and follow.

LOVE, FOLLOW, REPEAT

One of the most essential things we can do for our children is love our spouses. What a difference that makes! And the very best thing we can do for them—and for all those around us, really—is to live out a passionate, fiery faith before them. Now there's something to follow. We can serve where they can see us, yes. But much more than service. The waves of the overwhelming busy demands of ministry can start to drown out our excitement for all things Jesus. When serving Christ drowns out enjoying the presence of Christ, it's time for us to follow a new path.

His presence—that's where our purpose is found, our joy, our energy for loving service, our satisfaction in life and more. And it makes choosing the path to enjoying His presence all the more urgent when we think of the fact that there are those who are following. I know it's basic Sunday School that Jesus must come first. And maybe I'm coming down a bit too heavy on the "repeat" of this particular reality, but activity can be so distracting. The enemy can use it to get us to settle for doing good works and checking off everything on our churchy to-do list, missing the vital, refreshing, life-giving connection with Jesus. I don't want to settle for that life path. And I certainly don't want to lead anyone else down it.

Paul said in 1 Corinthians 11:1, "Follow my example, as I follow the example of Christ" (NIV). As long as we're zealously following Jesus, we don't have to work ourselves into a lather about our kids. If we love Jesus and love and respect His church, there's a good chance they will follow.

FOLLOW-THROUGH

In the day-to-day dealings of life in the ministry, it's right for us to protect our children from some of the upheaval we might experience. It's also OK to let people know that it's our responsibility to raise our children, not the church's.

I remember well the first time someone said to me, "I expected more of the pastor's kid." I responded very simply, "He doesn't get special spiritual powers because he's the pastor's kid. It doesn't make him an adult either. So I would appreciate it if you would help me let everyone know that we want him to be able just to be a kid."

It may seem like I was being snarky, but honestly, I didn't say it with any animosity whatsoever. I told her my son and his parents were sinners just like everyone else and merely asked her to give him room to make some dumb kid moves. And she responded well. Sometimes they will, sometimes they won't.

SOME PERSONAL FOLLOW-UP

I will tell you that I have *not* parented my children perfectly. I've made tons of missteps—probably overprotected them at points and underprotected them at others. But I'm happy to report . . . grace! So much grace. All five of my children follow Christ.

I have a better vantage point now. Just a few weeks ago we hit a milestone. All my kids are now officially out of their teens. How did that happen? Yet here we are, out the other side of raising our babies.

As of this writing, my oldest son, Andy, has traveled far and wide as a full-time *musicianary* (his word—and I love it), writing, recording and leading music all over the world. Jordan, my second-born son, is finishing up his seminary degree in pastoral studies, his master of divinity degree, and serving on staff at a megachurch between the studies. My oldest daughter, Kaley, is active in ministry and writes Christian fiction with me. Allie, my youngest daughter, recently married an amazing, Jesus-loving man, and she serves on staff at the same church where my youngest son, Daniel, serves as worship pastor. Daniel is the one who just turned 20, and this past week he popped the question to the precious girl to whom I dedicated this book.

Honestly, I don't share this to brag. I take credit for how amazing they are when I'm talking to people who don't know me. I can't get away with it with people who do know me, though. They're the ones who know without a doubt that I had very little at all to do with it.

I truly do know it's not because of my great parenting. I hesitated to add my kid report, worrying that it would sound a little "all about me" or "look what I did." But I'm praying the Lord will let you see my heart—that He would use this sharing to encourage you. I messed up. Lots. And my kids are not actually any closer to perfect than I am. We've had our share of upheaval here and there. I also realize that anything could happen in the future. But I wanted to hearten you with the knowledge that even though I botched things up in all kinds of directions—and then repeated *that*—still my children survived it. And they survived it with their love of Christ and the love and respect of His church still intact. It's a big love that shows up in the way they all serve Christ with great passion. It really does happen.

The bottom line: follow Jesus so intimately that when your kids follow you, it's a good thing. And then rest in His grace.

As for the instruction labels, I would encourage you to follow most of those too. Including the one on the mattress that said, "Do not attempt to swallow."

P-Dub to P-Dub with DEANNA SELF

Wouldn't you like to have a few do-overs regarding raising your kids? Years ago, our youngest daughter was having some issues with her friends at church and wanted to take some time off from the missions program, but her Dad and I made her go anyway. But if I could have a do-over, I would have let her have some space for a while.

Looking back, where was the catastrophe? In that moment, things seemed bigger than they do today. Are you thinking, "What's the big deal? Don't we *all* have to be around people that we don't want to be at times?" Well, from my daughter's perspective, it was a big deal. What's sad is that while trying to "keep the peace" at church for adults, which was and is impossible, our own daughter's peace was sacrificed.

We can't erase the past, but we can go forward. Bless your child by admitting your part, share your perspective, and validate hers. Communicate regrets. Then give yourself a break! You can't be a perfect parent any more than your child can be a perfect child. Only Christ is perfect. Shield them going forward. And grow them with your unending love and hugs.

P-DUB PARTNER-LINK: http://www.youtube.com /watch?v=Zl7-E3HaJAs

You can find an easy link at rhondarhea.com at the P-Dub tab.

P-DUB POSTSCRIPTS

Passages to Plug In

Brethren, together follow my example and observe those who live after the pattern we have set for you" (Philippians 3:17 AMP).

And you [set yourselves to] *become imitators of us and* [through us] *of the Lord Himself, for you welcomed our message in* [spite of] *much persecution, with joy* [inspired] *by the Holy Spirit"* (1 Thessalonians 1:6 AMP).

For you yourselves know how it is necessary to imitate our example, for we were not disorderly or shirking of duty when we were with you [we were not idle]. . . . [It was] *not because we do not have a right* [to such support], *but [we wished] to make ourselves an example for you to follow"* (2 Thessalonians 3:7, 9 AMP).

Ponderings to Pose

Have you "dropped your nets" to follow His instructions? Are you passionately repeating? And at every failure are you grabbing on to His grace? Deanna Self gives us a wise and practical outline for how to deal with our parenting failures. Ready to plug these in when the need arises?

• Admit your part
• Share your perspective /
• Validate your child's perspective
• Communicate regrets
• Give yourself a break

Petitions to Pray

Proverbs 20:7 says, "The righteous who walks in his integrity—blessed are his children after him!" (ESV). Ask the Lord to help you stay eagerly, wholeheartedly enthusiastic in the way you follow Him, walking with integrity for your children to see. Then pray for your children to experience the amazing blessing of following Him as well.

CHAPTER 26

I'll Come by and Pick You Up

Sometimes you just need to hear that you're going to be OK. Encouragement, p-dub to p-dub.

SEVERAL YEARS AGO THE CHURCH where we were serving called a new worship pastor. His wife? Cute as a button. But, being the spiritual giant that I am, I loved her loads anyway. They had two small children at the time—also adorable.

It was apparent from the get-go that Kristy had a big heart and a great spirit of adventure. Her very first Sunday in our new and maybe even slightly intimidating church, my husband was preaching on marriage. At the end of the service, he invited those who would like to pray for the marriages of our church to come forward. Kristy-big-heart popped up immediately to pray.

What she didn't realize was that somewhere near the first of the service, she had sat on her daughter's sucker. Her daughter's freshly power-licked, heart-shaped, red sucker. Giant sucker. White suit. Oh my. Kristy was kneeling for prayer there at the front of the worship center. The congregation got the full-on rear view.

The front four or five pews were filled with teenagers. My oldest son was around 14 at the time. He came up to me after the service with a "Mom, did Mrs. Ford know that she had a sucker stuck on her . . . um . . . *dress*?"

One of the other pastor's wives was already helping her pry the thing off by the time I got to her. Of course, I wouldn't even consider mentioning the ordeal to the poor girl. No, I considered her feelings and let the whole thing slide.

Yeah, right.

There were so many jokes to be made, I didn't even know where to start. I was so wishing I'd made it to her in time to sing in my Kindergarten sing-songy voice, "I know something you don't know."

HER HEART WAS IN THE RIGHT PLACE

Kristy had a big heart all right. And I'm not talking about the sucker. The girl knew how to have a good laugh—even at herself. She knew how to be gracious, even when it turned out she just might be the butt of a church sucker joke for a few years.

Not everyone is so gracious. Some wear their hearts on their sleeves. Kristy? Not at all. As a matter of fact, that particular day she wore hers on her rear end. In front of the entire church. And instead of starting in on the gazillion jokes begging to be made, I put my arm around her and said in my most official senior-pastor's-wife's-pronouncement voice: "You are now . . . one of us."

I wish I'd thought to dub her royal-style with the red sucker, one shoulder, then the other, but I didn't think of it until later. That's OK. It was already a sweet moment. With or without a power-lick.

THE REAL HEART OF THE MATTER

Sometimes we need that reminder that we're not in this alone. Other women have found themselves in those "sticky" situations. Some funny. Some not so funny. Some positively heartbreaking. We need that arm around the shoulder. We need to know that we're not alone. And we need to know without a shadow of a doubt that the Lord will be our strength when we have none. And He is our joy—our reason to laugh.

> *The Lord is my strength and my shield; my heart trusts in Him, and I am helped. Therefore my heart rejoices, and I praise Him with my song. The Lord is the strength of His people; He is a stronghold of salvation for His anointed* (Psalm 28:7–8).

It's my hope that this book has been and will continue to be not only a reminder of the great God who is your strength, but also your "arm around the shoulder." You're not alone.

Let's continue to encourage each other to stick to Jesus. And then stick to each other. Sticky sisters of the heart.

P-Dub to P-Dub with DAWN WILSON

At my first in-home event as a young pastor's wife, I made yummy foods, arranged flowers for the table and purchased "spring fling" plates to coordinate my theme for a group of ladies.

But in the middle of my party, I just about choked on a frosted daisy cookie when I overheard one lady whispering to another. "Tacky," she said. "Paper plates! Just tacky. What was she thinking?" This was my introduction to being a pastor's wife. It didn't matter that I could teach a Bible study and counsel the flock. I had the audacity to use paper plates. My shame was a sign of struggles to come.

I was never right and never enough. I couldn't be omnipresent. I struggled walking the fine line between meek and sweet versus confident and bold. Some women thought I should be more involved, especially in the nursery. Others didn't want me poking my nose into "the work of the church." In less than a year, my joy in ministry vanished.

I had Jesus, but oh, how I longed for a girlfriend—so hungry for encouragement. Today, many years later, I lead a group designed to encourage women in ministry. I've learned we *need* each other, especially when the craziness of ministry conspires to shut us down.

P-DUB PARTNER-LINK: http://youtu.be/uxbzuqVLDJs

You can find an easy link at rhondarhea.com at the P-Dub tab.

P-DUB POSTSCRIPTS

Passages to Plug In

For this reason I kneel before the Father from whom every family in heaven and on earth is named. I pray that He may grant you, according to the riches of His glory, to be strengthened with power in the inner man through His Spirit, and that the Messiah may dwell in your hearts through faith. I pray that you, being rooted and firmly established in love, may be able to comprehend with all the saints what is the length and width, height and depth of God's love, and to know the Messiah's love that surpasses knowledge, so you may be filled with all the fullness of God (Ephesians 3:14–19).

Ponderings to Pose

Dawn understands in the most personal way the need for connection. Sometimes we do need someone to talk to or giggle with. We need someone who "gets us" to offer a word of counsel or wisdom. Or we just need to know we're not in this alone. Dawn recognized the need and later the Lord called her to lead a group for women in ministry. Could the Lord be calling you to be a part of that kind of group? Or maybe even lead out in one?

Petitions to Pray

My dear p-dub friends, I'm hoping that one of the grain-messages you're able to glean from this book is—let me say it one more time—you really are not in this alone. We do get each other. With that in mind, in this last "Petitions to Pray" section, I would love the honor of praying for *you*, my sister of the heart.

Heavenly Father, thank You for my sister. Thank you for the calling You've placed on her life. I pray You will bless her in that calling, and that You will grant her amazing, surprising, blessed fruit. Lord, I pray she would be encouraged in loving her husband and in coming alongside him in ministry. Bless every big ministry and every little ministry You're calling her to. Thank You that we can know You will faithfully give her absolutely everything she needs to accomplish all that You're calling her to do. Meet her every need by Your grace and through Your mercy.

I also ask, Lord, that You would use the testimonies and messages of this book to be an "arm around the shoulder" of my p-dub girlfriend. Father, may she feel a camaraderie. A connection. A sweet sisterhood. Thank You for our p-dub community. Every time it's needed, I pray You'll grant her a true friend—whether it's long-distance or up-close-and-personal. I pray You will ease feelings of loneliness and soothe every hurt. Heal her heart in those hurting places. Strengthen every weak place. Help her to continue to grow as a pastor's wife, but mostly simply to continue to grow as a follower of Your Son.

Father, let us stick to You. And stick together. May our shoulder-to-shoulder connection strengthen us in Your love.

By Your grace and for Your glory, in the name of Jesus, Amen.

P-Dub Contributor Bios

BETSY BARTIG and her husband, Matt, have been married for 16 years. They have two wonderful boys, Micah and Jonah. Betsy and Matt began working in student ministry during their college days at Hannibal LaGrange University in Hannibal, Missouri, and since then, the Lord has led them all over the country to minister in every size church imaginable. They're now taking a new step of faith in service as church planters in Moscow Mills, Missouri, the North American Mission Board's "send city." Betsy and Matt are looking forward to this new chapter in their lives.

ROBIN BRYCE is a speaker and writer encouraging ministers and those who want to be in nontraditional ministry. Her soon-to-be-released project offers creative ministers help with some entrepreneurial principles. She's a pastor's wife, mother of three, and "Nisi" to one. Her Texas home is full of laughter, half-baked ideas, and full-blown critters. To have her speak for your event, check out RobinBryce.com/speaking.

DIANE CAMPBELL is the wife of Brent Campbell, director of missions for the Twin Rivers Baptist Association in the St. Louis area. She has worked many years in prison ministries and deaf ministries and teaches Bible studies to all kinds of groups. Diane is the mother of two grown children and teaches third grade at the First Baptist Christian Academy in Troy, Missouri.

BOBBYE CUTSHALL and her pastor/husband, Art, have been in the ministry for 22 years. She has a degree in early childhood education and has directed several related ministries and spent many years teaching college childcare classes. Bobbye's first love is discipling women and teens to bring them to a close personal relationship with the Savior. Bobbye and Art live in Muscatine, Iowa.

JOYCE DINKINS and husband, Steven, joined by their three adult children, recently paid tribute to God while celebrating 25 years of marriage and ministry. Joyce joined New Hope Publishers as managing editor in 2006, following service with NavPress and David C. Cook, where Steven served as a bivocational minister, in national sales management. With a passion for serving alongside urban pastors, Steven is on Destiny Covenant Church's pastoral team in Birmingham, Alabama, at this writing. He previously served as an associate pastor with New City, Colorado Springs, and Christ Community Church, Chicago. People lovers, Bible teachers, and speakers, they engage in missions, including in East Africa and Haiti.

SANDEE HEDGER is the wife of Dr. Rick Hedger, who serves as team leader for missions & evangelism as well as partnership mission specialist for the Missouri Baptist Convention. Sandee and Rick come to their current assignment in mission mobilization following 29 years in local church ministry, where Dr. Hedger served as senior pastor of churches in Arkansas, Missouri, and Tennessee. Sandee is an avid Bible teacher and serves regularly as keynote speaker for women's conferences and retreats around the globe. Her thirst to "know Christ intimately, and make Him known clearly" is the driving force of her leadership in women's discipleship and missional service. The Hedgers are parents of two young adult children, Joshua and Kaila, both serving in ministry and missions. They reside in Jefferson City, Missouri.

JAMIE HITT is a devoted wife of 30 years to Greg Hitt and was a stay-at-home/homeschooling mom of three children, now grown. She is a diligent student of the Bible and a professional musician. Jamie holds a bachelor of music education degree with an emphasis in voice and has been singing alongside her husband for more than 20 years, ministering in churches, conventions, conferences, National Day of Prayer events, Missouri Legislative prayer events, and more. She is known to the Missouri Baptist Convention as a music evangelist and held the office of Recording Secretary with the Executive Board for four years. Jamie and Greg now live in Amarillo, Texas.

SHARON HOFFMAN's mission statement is, "Challenging women to change their world!" A speaker/author known for her warm demeanor and trademark smile, this vivacious woman has spoken to audiences throughout the United States, Canada, and overseas for more than 25 years. Sharon is the author of *The GIFTed Woman, Come Home to Comfort, Untie the Ribbons, The Today Girl*, and *A Car Seat in My Convertible*. A lover of chocolate, gardening, and hiking, Sharon has touched many lives through her vulnerability and powerful life story. This amazing woman wears many hats, including wife, mother, grandmom, pastor's wife, and Baptist Bible college dean of women. She and her husband, Rob, call Springfield, Missouri home.

CYNTHIA HOPKINS is the author of the very funny and poignant blog *Blog in My Eye,* enjoyed by both women and men of all ages. Cynthia has been writing articles, devotions and curriculum for LifeWay Christian Resources for more than 13 years. She also enjoys speaking to women's groups and youth events. She has a unique wit that keeps people laughing. She uses that, along with her love for God's Word and her realness, to point people to Jesus. Cynthia is married to Clay, who serves on staff at First Baptist Church of Midlothian, Texas, as high school pastor. They have been married 23 years and have two teenagers, Brandon and Abby. Find Cynthia's blog, along with more information at cynthiahopkins.org.

NICOLE HUFTY is partner to her husband, Zac, and parent to two toddler daughters. She is passionate about sharing Christ to the next generation. She and her husband have served in youth ministry for the past 10 years and are currently serving at Houston's First Baptist Church where Zac is student minister. Part-time accountant and full-time mommy, when she's not

loving on her husband or girls, Nicole enjoys coffee, being out-
doors, reading and planning their next vacation. Follow her on
Twitter @NicoleHufty and their blog at thehuftys.blogspot.com.

KELLY LIGHTFOOT has always had a love of everything creative
and has owned her own graphic design business, Ampersand,
since 2010. When she's not cooking up new recipes, Kelly and
her husband, Andrew, can often be found around a campfire or
in downtown Kansas City for an evening stroll or local dining.

DEB MASHBURN and her husband, Brad, are missionaries
in West Africa working among the rural poor. They have five
children, two natural and three adopted from Sierra Leone. Deb
is also a pastor's daughter, has a chemistry degree, and never
thought she'd be a missionary. It seems, though, to be what
God intended all along.

ROBIN MCCALL is passionate about teaching young women
about abiding in God's grace and mercy and love, and the joy
of living a Spirit-filled life. She is the wife of Bill McCall, pastor
of the Baptist Church at McAdory in McCalla, Alabama. She
and her husband live on a farm with their two sons, Sam and
Will, and an ever evolving menagerie. When she's not serving
at church or working on the farm, she edits preschool resources
at national Woman's Missionary Union.

JANET MCGLAUGHLIN is Missouri-born-and-raised and
graduated from Southwest Baptist College and Southwest
Missouri State. An elementary school teacher for 36 years, Janet
has also worked in the Parents as First Teachers program. She
enjoys ministries with children, youth and adults, teaching
Bible studies and has also served in many missions, Vacation
Bible Schools, and camp programs. Janet has also loved
counseling and teaching Bible studies in women's prisons for
the past 15 years. She is married to L. Douglas McGlaughlin,
who has served as pastor for 52 years.

LORI MOODY has been married to Scott Moody, a pastor, for 32 years. They have three grown children and one grandson. Lori leads the women's ministry at First Baptist Church Silsbee, Texas, where she has served for 17 years. Her hobbies include spending time with family, reading, and crocheting.

PAULA MOWERY is a pastor's wife and a homeschooling mom. She has written three Bible studies and is a columnist for *Christian Online Magazine* (christianonlinemagazine.com). You can find out more about her ministry, including her novella, *The Blessing Seer* (Pelican Ventures Book Group—Harbourlight Books, 2012), at paulamowery.blogspot.com.

MARY ENGLUND MURPHY and her husband, Bill, have been in church ministry for more than 40 years serving in both small and large congregations. Born into a blended family and surviving cancer, Mary has used her personal struggles to minister to women of all ages in the church and at retreats. She and her husband live in Tulsa, Oklahoma. Find out more about Mary at lookingglassministries.com.

DIANE NIX is the wife of Dr. Preston L. Nix, who pastored for 21 years, now director of the Landrum Leavell School of Evangelism and a professor at New Orleans Baptist Theological Seminary. Diane is the spiritual mom of two grown daughters and the biological mom of two teenagers. Diane shares inspiring stories of victory through adversity, including losing everything she owned in Hurricane Katrina only three weeks after moving there. She has an amazing testimony as well of surviving a difficult battle with meningitis 10 months after Katrina. Find out more about her inspirational journey of never giving up at dianenix.com.

KATIE ORR is a grace-clinger. Truth-speaker. Pastor's wife. Mommy of three. Auburn fan. Katie Orr loves to equip others to walk with God. Through her speaking and writing ministries, she is honored to teach others how to hear from God through His Word. You can learn more about Katie and her ministry at KatieOrr.me, and you can always find her hanging out on Twitter as @KatieOrr22.

DEANNA SELF is a licensed professional counselor in private practice in St. Charles County, Missouri, specializing in individual, marriage, couple and family therapy. She holds an MA in counseling and an MA in general theology from Covenant Theological Seminary. Deanna is a pastor's wife and mother of two married children and grandmother of four. She serves in various music and leadership ministries at her church.

STEPHANIE SHOTT is an author, a popular international speaker and the founder of The M.O.M. Initiative, a missional mentoring ministry dedicated to taking Titus 2 to the streets. For more than 20 years, Stephanie has led women to live full, fearless and faithful lives. Her Bible study on Ecclesiastes, *Understanding What Matters Most,* is a favorite of women everywhere. She has also written for *P31 Woman Magazine, MOPS International, Focus on the Family* and many more. Stephanie lives in Jacksonville, Florida, and you can find out more about her at stephanieshott. com or visit themominitiative.com. You can also connect with Stephanie on Facebook and Twitter.

KATHY THARP is the wife and life adventure partner to Jerry, who is a great husband, amazing dad, grandpa, and a pastor. They have four children and three adorable grandchildren. One of their life adventures took them to Brazil where they served as church planting missionaries for 12 years. While in Brazil, besides homeschooling her children and handling the responsibilities as missionary, Kathy also worked at an English language school. Upon their return to the United States in 1999, she continued as a curriculum developer and editor for the school. Kathy is now the international program director for Summit Christian Academy and continues to write and edit in various capacities and languages. She is an international speaker and vocalist who enjoys encouraging women around the world to discover all that God has for them.

CHARLYN THOMASSON has been the main support for her pastor/husband, David, more than 30 years. She has two grown sons, a daughter-in-law, and a granddaughter. Her favorite places are the beach, sidewalk cafes, boutiques, bookstores, and Starbucks! Charlyn's favorite pastime is meaningful and fun conversation with family and friends. She lives in Jacksonville, Florida, and is a life purpose coach, image consultant, and founder of The True You—Image & Coaching, thetrueyou.net.

TERI LYNNE UNDERWOOD is a Word lover and idea slinger. A passionate encourager of rest, focus, and embracing life's seasons, she tries to make time every day for good coffee, excellent books, and lingering conversations. Whether writing or speaking, Teri Lynne's greatest passion is offering women permission to live well. As a pastor's wife and a cheerleader's mom, Teri Lynne is typically three days behind on laundry and trying to remember where she's supposed to be next. Lately the Lord has been teaching her a lot of lessons about humility, listening, and loving others well. Teri Lynne lives in Russellville, Alabama, and you can find out more about her and her ministries at terilynneunderwood.com.

DAWN WILSON, founder of Heart Choices Ministries, also serves as San Diego chapter president for the Network of Evangelical Women in Ministry (NEWIM), and blogs at UpgradeWithDawn.com, encouraging women to make wise, biblical choices. She coauthored the devotional *LOL with God* with Pam Farrel. Dawn and her husband, Bob, have two married sons and three granddaughters, and have served together in three churches and two ministries for more than four decades.

New Hope® Publishers is a division of WMU®, an international organization that challenges Christian believers to understand and be radically involved in God's mission. For more information about WMU, go to wmu.com. More information about New Hope books may be found at NewHopeDigital.com. New Hope books may be purchased at your local bookstore.

Use the QR reader on your smartphone to visit us online at NewHopeDigital.com

If you've been blessed by this book, we would like to hear your story. The publisher and author welcome your comments and suggestions at: newhopereader@wmu.org.

Other Books by this Author...

Expresso Your Faith
30 Shots of God's Word to Keep You Focused on Christ
ISBN-13: 978-1-59669-366-1
N134109 $14.99

How Many Lightbulbs Does It Take to Change a Person?
Bright Ideas for Delightful Transformation
ISBN-13: 978-1-59669-325-8
N124132 • $14.99

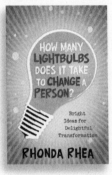

Available in bookstores everywhere.
For information about these books or this author, visit
NewHopeDigital.com.

Experience New Hope Women in Bible Study!
A new digital Bible Study community to help encourage, equip, and engage your walk with Christ in your ministry. New Hope Women in Bible Study provides fresh articles, and topical content for every woman, interactive Bible study workbooks that allow you to take your Bible study with you wherever you go, and the chance to engage with New Hope's world-renowned Bible study authors on topics such as prayer, discipleship, marriage, and more! Visit today! NewHopeDigital.com/women